EYEWITNESS VISUAL DICTIONARIES

THE VISUAL
DICTIONARY *of*
ANIMALS

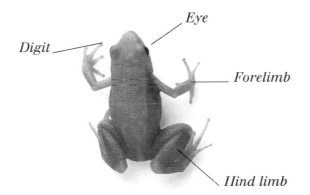

Eye

Digit

Forelimb

Hind limb

**EXTERNAL FEATURES
OF A FROG**

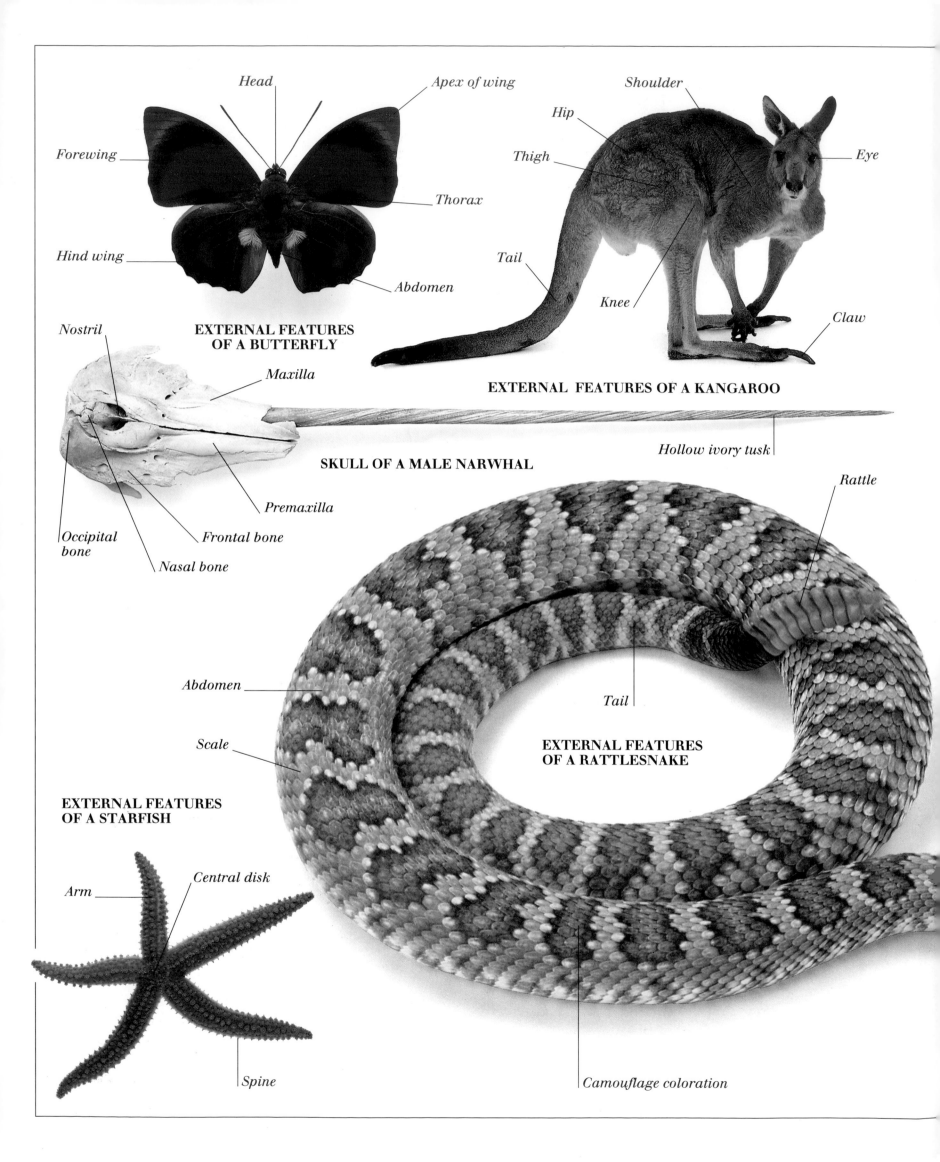

Head

Apex of wing

Shoulder

Hip

Thigh

Eye

Forewing

Thorax

Tail

Hind wing

Knee

Claw

Abdomen

**EXTERNAL FEATURES
OF A BUTTERFLY**

EXTERNAL FEATURES OF A KANGAROO

Nostril

Maxilla

Hollow ivory tusk

SKULL OF A MALE NARWHAL

Rattle

Premaxilla

Occipital
bone

Frontal bone

Nasal bone

Abdomen

Tail

**EXTERNAL FEATURES
OF A RATTLESNAKE**

Scale

**EXTERNAL FEATURES
OF A STARFISH**

Central disk

Arm

Spine

Camouflage coloration

EYEWITNESS VISUAL DICTIONARIES

THE VISUAL
DICTIONARY *of*
ANIMALS

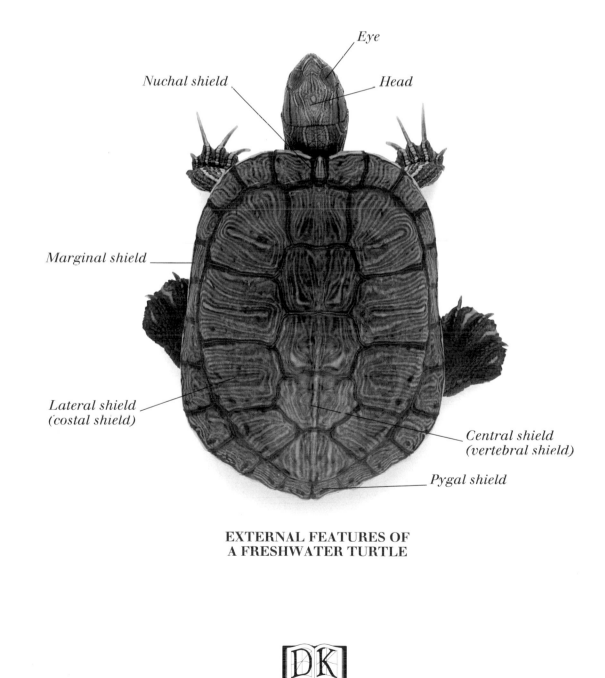

Eye

Nuchal shield

Head

Marginal shield

Lateral shield
(costal shield)

Central shield
(vertebral shield)

Pygal shield

**EXTERNAL FEATURES OF
A FRESHWATER TURTLE**

DK

A DK PUBLISHING BOOK

PROJECT ART EDITOR CLARE SHEDDEN
DESIGNER ANDREW NASH

PROJECT EDITOR MARTYN PAGE
CONSULTANT EDITOR DR RICHARD WALKER

SERIES ART EDITOR PAUL WILKINSON
ART DIRECTOR CHEZ PICTHALL
MANAGING EDITOR RUTH MIDGLEY

PHOTOGRAPHY DAVE KING, GEOFF DANN
ILLUSTRATIONS JOHN WOODCOCK, SIMONE END

PRODUCTION HILARY STEPHENS

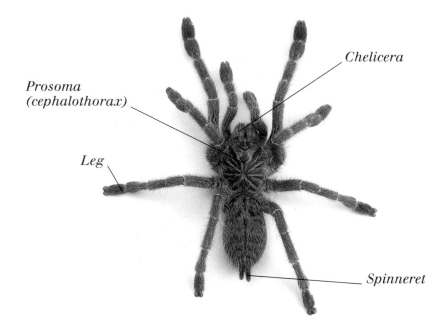

Chelicera

*Prosoma
(cephalothorax)*

Leg

Spinneret

EXTERNAL FEATURES OF A SPIDER

FIRST AMERICAN EDITION, 1991

10 9

DK PUBLISHING, INC., 95 MADISON AVENUE
NEW YORK, NEW YORK, 10016

COPYRIGHT © 1991 DORLING KINDERSLEY LIMITED, LONDON

ALL RIGHTS RESERVED UNDER INTERNATIONAL AND PAN-AMERICAN COPYRIGHT CONVENTIONS.
PUBLISHED IN THE UNITED STATES BY DK PUBLISHING, INC., NEW YORK, NEW YORK
DISTRIBUTED BY HOUGHTON MIFFLIN COMPANY, BOSTON, MASSACHUSETTS.
NO PART OF THIS PUBLICATION MAY BE REPRODUCED, STORED IN A RETRIEVAL SYSTEM,
OR TRANSMITTED IN ANY FORM OR BY ANY MEANS, ELECTRONIC, MECHANICAL, PHOTOCOPYING, RECORDING,
OR OTHERWISE, WITHOUT THE PRIOR WRITTEN PERMISSION OF THE COPYRIGHT OWNER. PUBLISHED IN
GREAT BRITAIN BY DORLING KINDERSLEY LIMITED, LONDON.

ISBN: 1-879431-19-X (TRADE EDITION)
ISBN: 1-879431-34-3 (LIBRARY EDITION)

VISIT US ON THE WORLD WIDE WEB AT
HTTP://WWW.DK.COM

LIBRARY OF CONGRESS CARD CATALOG NUMBER: 91-60901

REPRODUCED BY GRB GRAFICA, VERONA, ITALY
PRINTED AND BOUND IN ITALY BY ARNOLDO MONDADORI, VERONA

Contents

Digit

Hind limb

Forelimb

EXTERNAL FEATURES OF A FROG

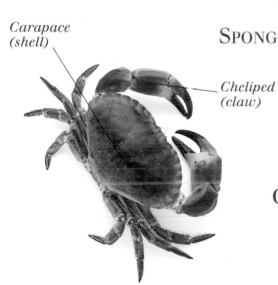

Carapace (shell)

Cheliped (claw)

EXTERNAL FEATURES OF A CRAB

Back

Eye

Forelimb

EXTERNAL FEATURES OF A RABBIT

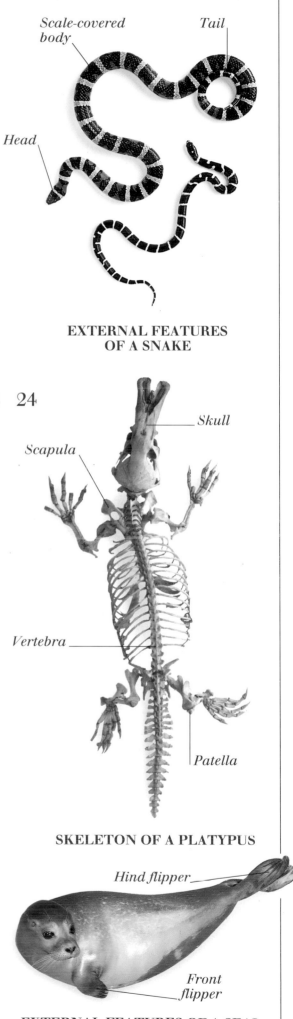

Scale-covered body

Tail

Head

EXTERNAL FEATURES OF A SNAKE

Skull

Scapula

Vertebra

Patella

SKELETON OF A PLATYPUS

Hind flipper

Front flipper

EXTERNAL FEATURES OF A SEAL

Animal bodies

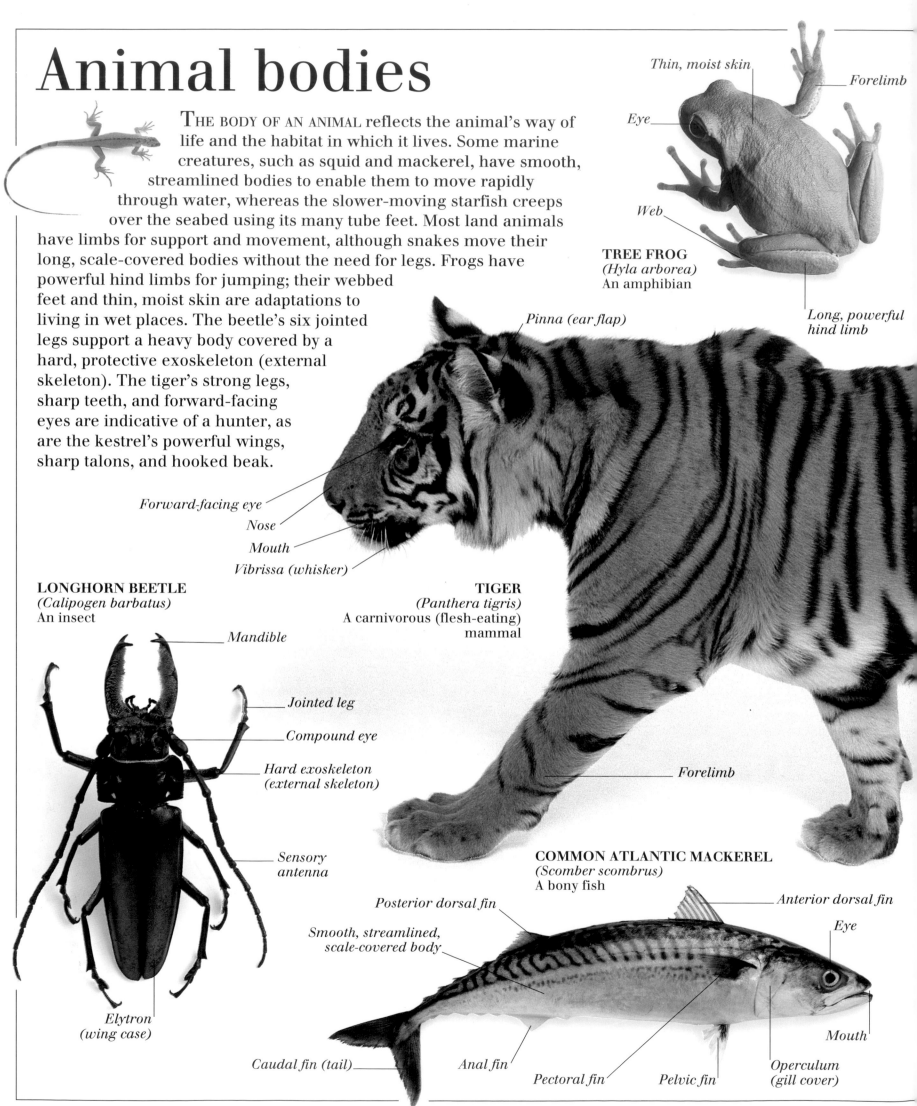

THE BODY OF AN ANIMAL reflects the animal's way of life and the habitat in which it lives. Some marine creatures, such as squid and mackerel, have smooth, streamlined bodies to enable them to move rapidly through water, whereas the slower-moving starfish creeps over the seabed using its many tube feet. Most land animals have limbs for support and movement, although snakes move their long, scale-covered bodies without the need for legs. Frogs have powerful hind limbs for jumping; their webbed feet and thin, moist skin are adaptations to living in wet places. The beetle's six jointed legs support a heavy body covered by a hard, protective exoskeleton (external skeleton). The tiger's strong legs, sharp teeth, and forward-facing eyes are indicative of a hunter, as are the kestrel's powerful wings, sharp talons, and hooked beak.

Thin, moist skin

Forelimb

Eye

Web

TREE FROG
(Hyla arborea)
An amphibian

Long, powerful hind limb

Pinna (ear flap)

Forward-facing eye

Nose

Mouth

Vibrissa (whisker)

LONGHORN BEETLE
(Calipogen barbatus)
An insect

TIGER
(Panthera tigris)
A carnivorous (flesh-eating)
mammal

Mandible

Jointed leg

Compound eye

*Hard exoskeleton
(external skeleton)*

*Sensory
antenna*

Forelimb

*Elytron
(wing case)*

COMMON ATLANTIC MACKEREL
(Scomber scombrus)
A bony fish

Posterior dorsal fin

Anterior dorsal fin

Eye

*Smooth, streamlined,
scale-covered body*

Caudal fin (tail)

Anal fin

Pectoral fin

Pelvic fin

Mouth

*Operculum
(gill cover)*

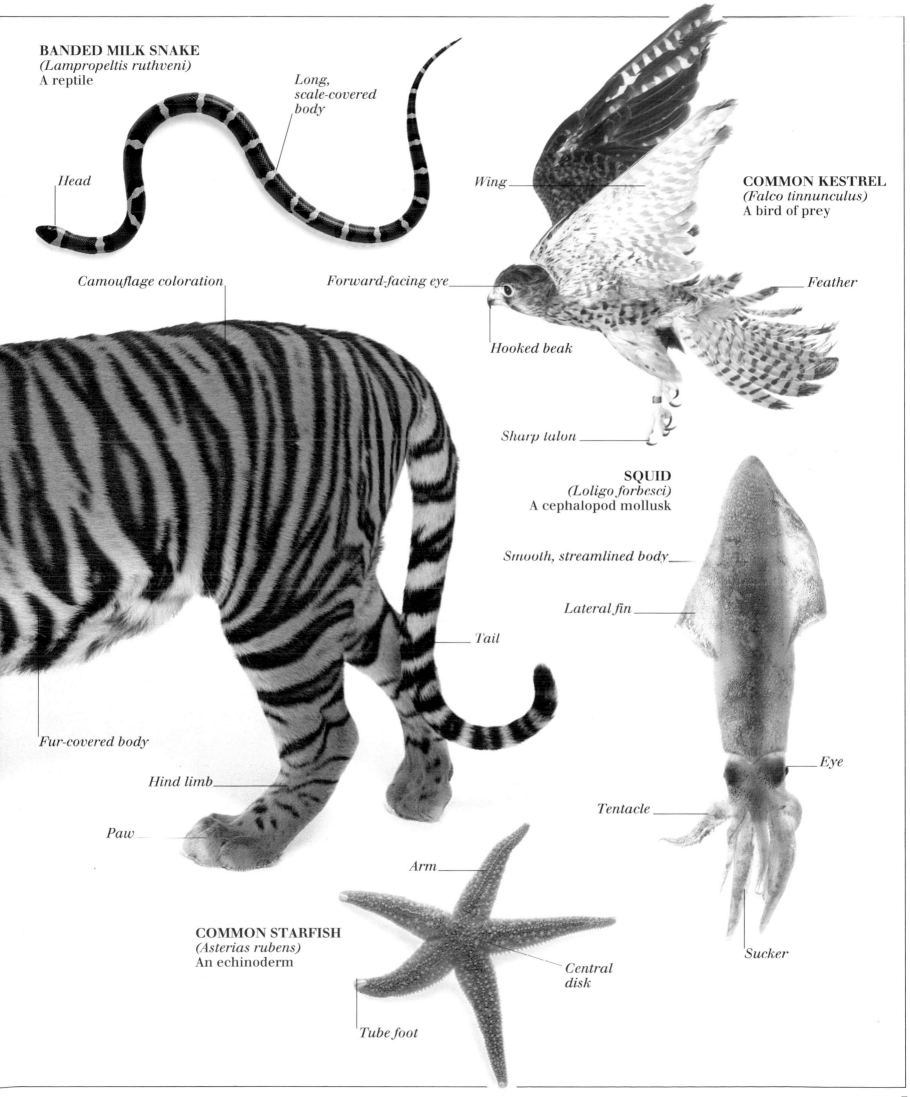

BANDED MILK SNAKE
(Lampropeltis ruthveni)
A reptile

Long, scale-covered body

Head

Camouflage coloration

COMMON KESTREL
(Falco tinnunculus)
A bird of prey

Wing

Forward-facing eye

Feather

Hooked beak

Sharp talon

SQUID
(Loligo forbesci)
A cephalopod mollusk

Smooth, streamlined body

Lateral fin

Tail

Eye

Fur-covered body

Tentacle

Hind limb

Paw

Arm

Sucker

COMMON STARFISH
(Asterias rubens)
An echinoderm

Central disk

Tube foot

Animal heads

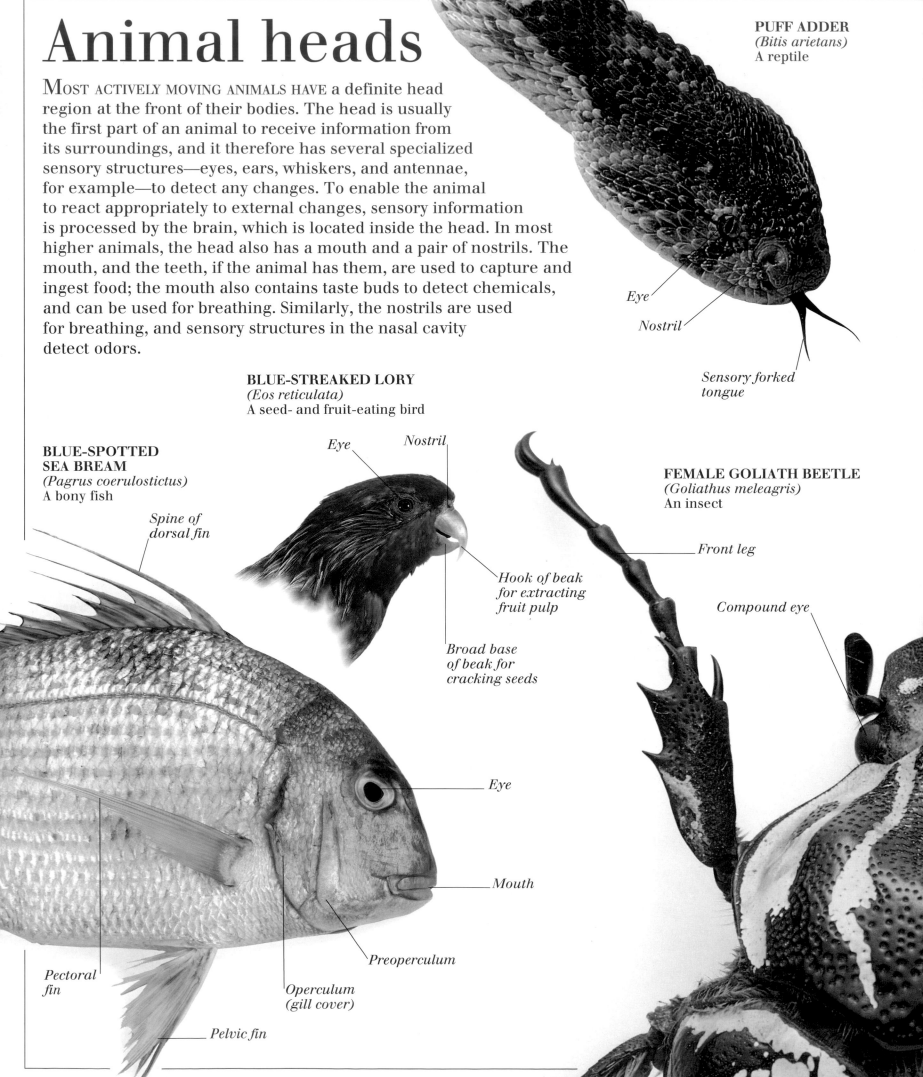

MOST ACTIVELY MOVING ANIMALS HAVE a definite head region at the front of their bodies. The head is usually the first part of an animal to receive information from its surroundings, and it therefore has several specialized sensory structures—eyes, ears, whiskers, and antennae, for example—to detect any changes. To enable the animal to react appropriately to external changes, sensory information is processed by the brain, which is located inside the head. In most higher animals, the head also has a mouth and a pair of nostrils. The mouth, and the teeth, if the animal has them, are used to capture and ingest food; the mouth also contains taste buds to detect chemicals, and can be used for breathing. Similarly, the nostrils are used for breathing, and sensory structures in the nasal cavity detect odors.

PUFF ADDER
(Bitis arietans)
A reptile

Eye

Nostril

Sensory forked tongue

BLUE-STREAKED LORY
(Eos reticulata)
A seed- and fruit-eating bird

Eye

Nostril

Hook of beak for extracting fruit pulp

Broad base of beak for cracking seeds

BLUE-SPOTTED SEA BREAM
(Pagrus coerulostictus)
A bony fish

Spine of dorsal fin

Eye

Mouth

Preoperculum

Operculum (gill cover)

Pelvic fin

Pectoral fin

FEMALE GOLIATH BEETLE
(Goliathus meleagris)
An insect

Front leg

Compound eye

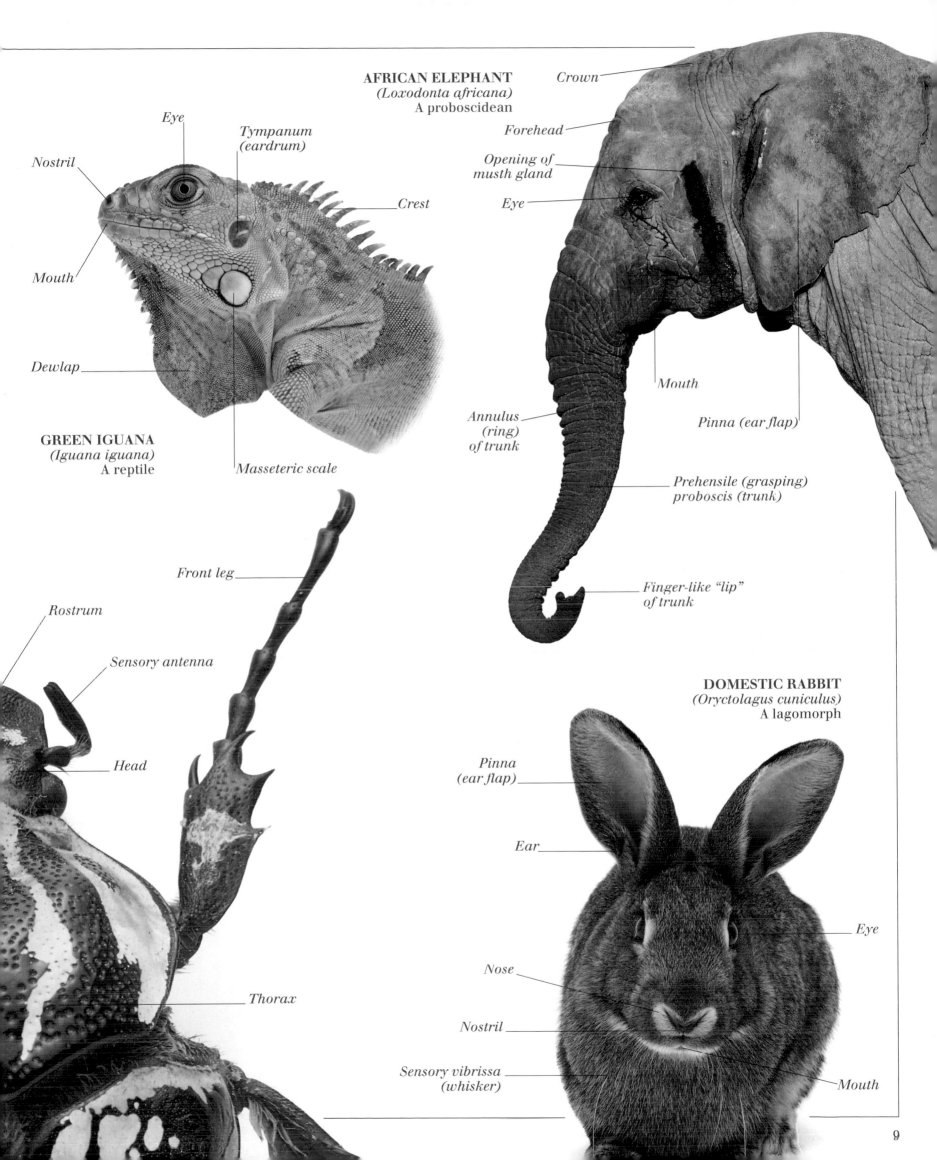

GREEN IGUANA
(Iguana iguana)
A reptile

Eye

Tympanum
(eardrum)

Nostril

Mouth

Crest

Dewlap

Masseteric scale

AFRICAN ELEPHANT
(Loxodonta africana)
A proboscidean

Crown

Forehead

Opening of
musth gland

Eye

Mouth

Pinna (ear flap)

Annulus
(ring)
of trunk

Prehensile (grasping)
proboscis (trunk)

Finger-like "lip"
of trunk

Front leg

Rostrum

Sensory antenna

Head

Thorax

DOMESTIC RABBIT
(Oryctolagus cuniculus)
A lagomorph

Pinna
(ear flap)

Ear

Eye

Nose

Nostril

Sensory vibrissa
(whisker)

Mouth

9

Butterflies and moths

BUTTERFLIES AND MOTHS FORM THE order Lepidoptera, one of the divisions of the large class Insecta, which is itself part of the even larger phylum Arthropoda. Lepidopterans are one of the biggest groups of insects, with about 150,000 species (which is about 15 percent of all known insects). They are characterized by having wings covered with tiny scales, hence the name of their order (Lepidoptera means "scale wings"). Butterflies and moths also possess features that are common to all insects: an exoskeleton (external skeleton); three pairs of jointed legs, although the front pair are very small in some lepidopterans; three body sections (head, thorax, and abdomen); and one pair of sensory antennae. Like certain other insects (beetles, flies, and bees, for example), butterflies and moths undergo complete metamorphosis during their life cycle.

DIFFERENCES BETWEEN BUTTERFLIES AND MOTHS

The separation of lepidopterans into butterflies and moths is largely artificial as there are no features that categorically distinguish one group from the other. In general, however, most butterflies fly by day, whereas most moths are night-flyers; butterflies tend to have clubbed antennae, whereas those of moths tend to be plain or feathery; butterflies usually rest with their wings upright over their backs, whereas moths rest with their wings flat; and butterflies tend to be more brightly colored than moths.

EXTERNAL FEATURES OF A BUTTERFLY

MOTH

Plain antenna

Dull-colored wings

BUTTERFLY

Clubbed antenna

Brightly colored wings

Antenna

Compound eye

Head

Proboscis

Foreleg

Thorax

Femur

Middle leg

Tibia

Hind leg

Tarsus

INTERNAL ANATOMY OF A FEMALE BUTTERFLY

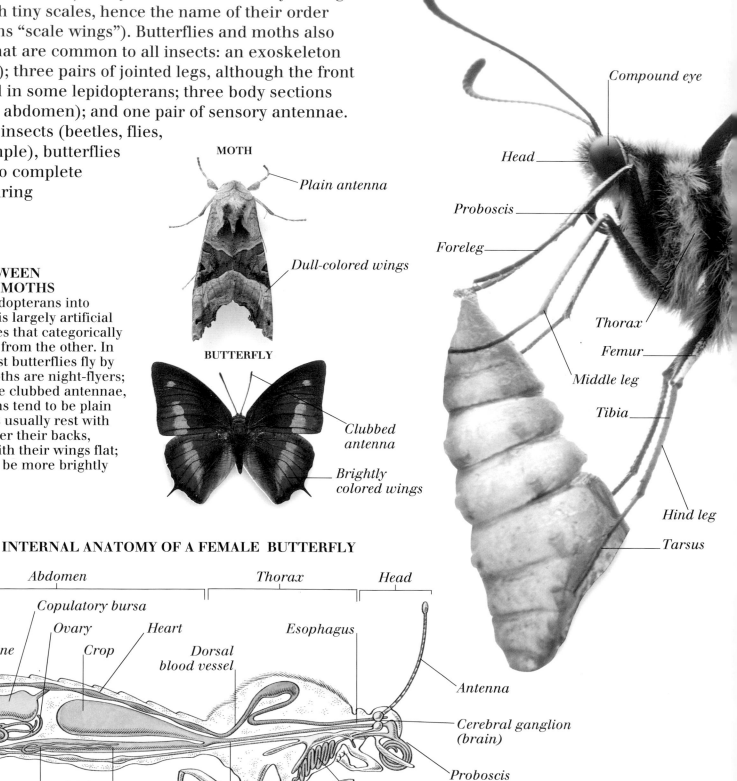

Abdomen

Thorax

Head

Copulatory bursa

Colon

Ovary

Heart

Esophagus

Rectum

Intestine

Crop

Dorsal blood vessel

Anus

Antenna

Cerebral ganglion (brain)

Proboscis

Oviduct

Midgut

Salivary gland

Opening of oviduct

Malpighian tubule

Seminal receptacle

Ventral nerve cord

Opening of copulatory bursa

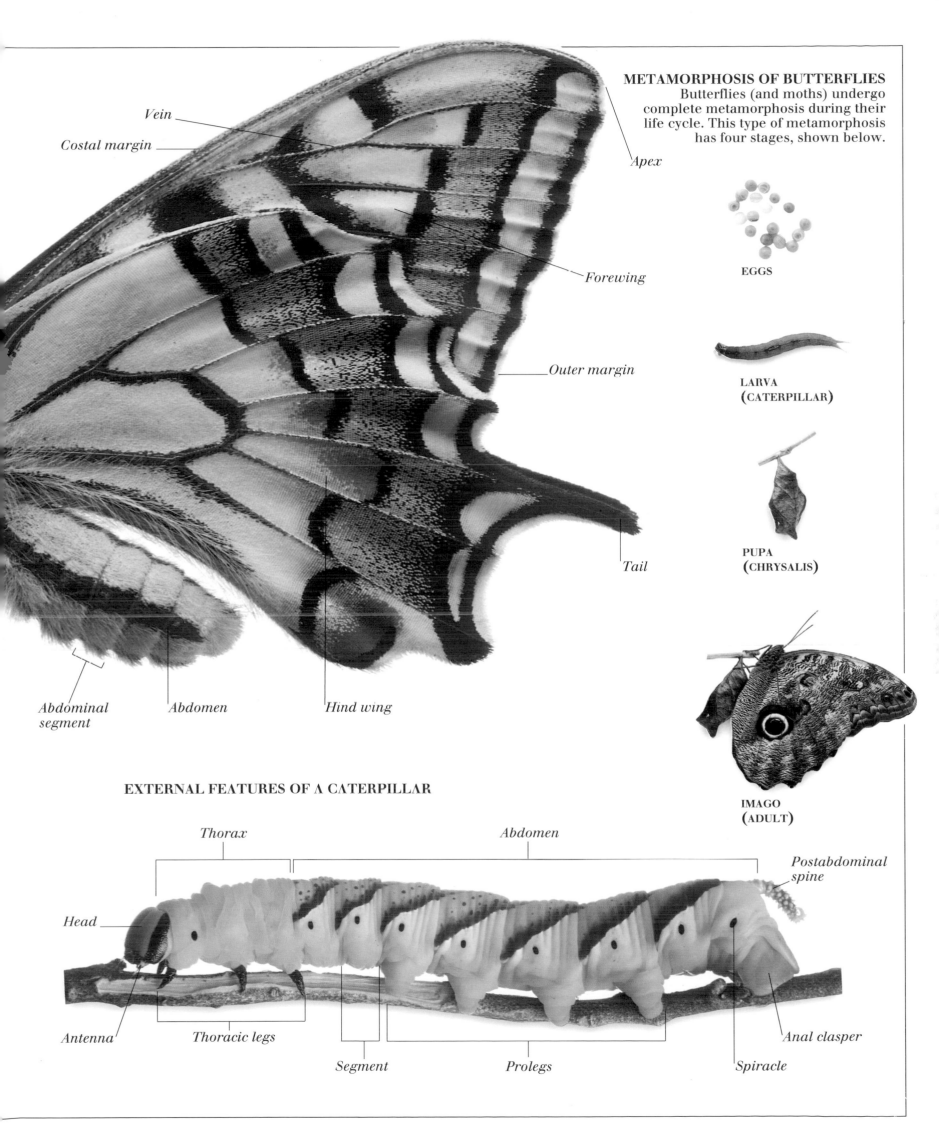

Vein

Costal margin

Apex

METAMORPHOSIS OF BUTTERFLIES
Butterflies (and moths) undergo complete metamorphosis during their life cycle. This type of metamorphosis has four stages, shown below.

EGGS

Forewing

LARVA
(CATERPILLAR)

Outer margin

PUPA
(CHRYSALIS)

Tail

Abdominal
segment

Abdomen

Hind wing

IMAGO
(ADULT)

EXTERNAL FEATURES OF A CATERPILLAR

Thorax

Abdomen

Postabdominal
spine

Head

Antenna

Thoracic legs

Segment

Prolegs

Anal clasper

Spiracle

Beetles, ants, and bees

BEETLES, ANTS, AND BEES BELONG to different orders in the class Insecta, which is a division of the phylum Arthropoda. Beetles (order Coleoptera) are the biggest group of insects, with about 300,000 species. The characteristic feature of beetles is a pair of hard elytra (wing cases), which are modified front wings. The principal function of the elytra is to protect the hind wings, which are used for flying. Ants, together with bees and wasps, form the order Hymenoptera, which contains about 200,000 species. This group is characterized by a marked narrowing between the thorax and abdomen. Both of the above groups also have features common to all insects: an exoskeleton (external skeleton); three pairs of jointed legs; three body sections (head, thorax, and abdomen); and one pair of sensory antennae.

TYPES OF BEES

Some bees (bumblebees and honeybees, for example) exhibit polymorphism, that is, different types (or castes) of bees occur in the same species. Bumblebees have three castes: workers, which are sterile females; drones, which are fertile males; and queens, which are fertile females.

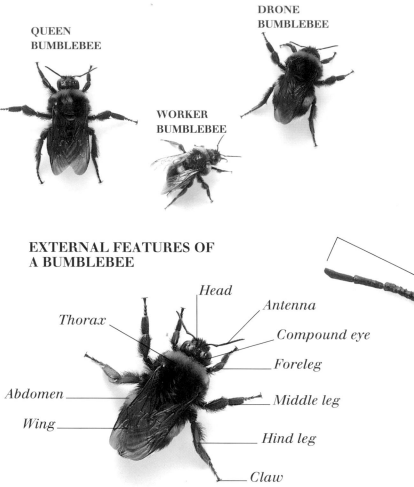

QUEEN BUMBLEBEE

DRONE BUMBLEBEE

WORKER BUMBLEBEE

EXTERNAL FEATURES OF A BUMBLEBEE

Head

Thorax

Antenna

Compound eye

Foreleg

Abdomen

Middle leg

Wing

Hind leg

Claw

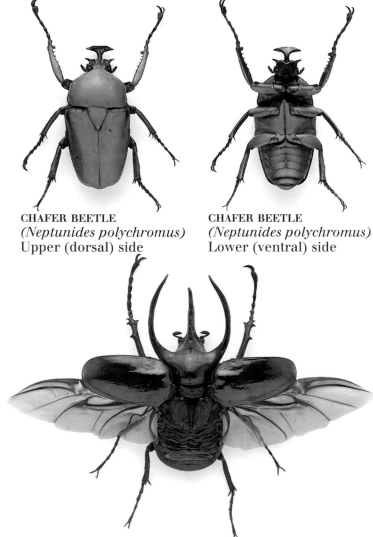

CHAFER BEETLE
(Neptunides polychromus)
Upper (dorsal) side

CHAFER BEETLE
(Neptunides polychromus)
Lower (ventral) side

EXAMPLES OF BEETLES

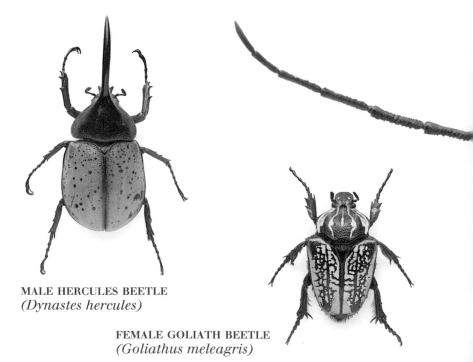

MALE ATLAS BEETLE
(Chalcosoma atlas)

MALE HERCULES BEETLE
(Dynastes hercules)

FEMALE GOLIATH BEETLE
(Goliathus meleagris)

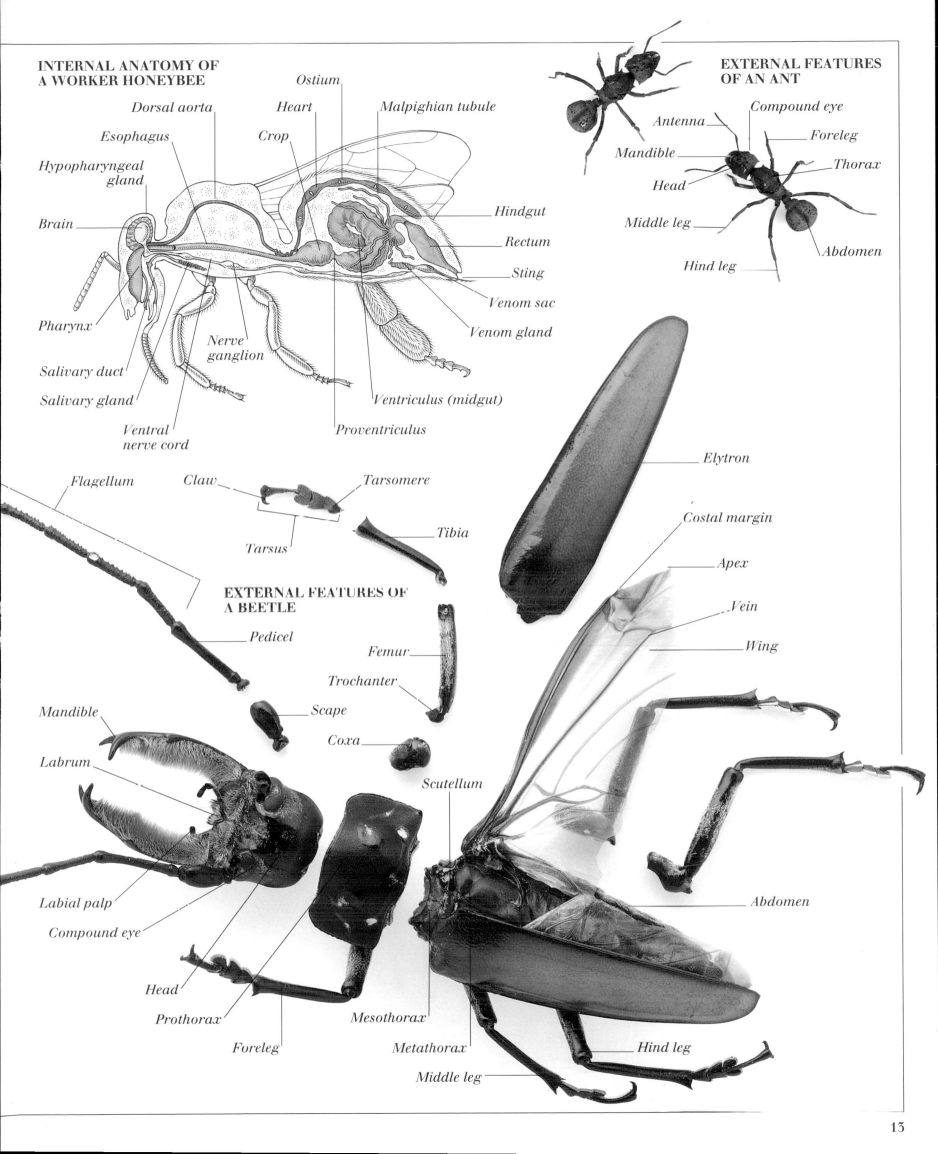

INTERNAL ANATOMY OF A WORKER HONEYBEE

Ostium
Dorsal aorta
Heart
Malpighian tubule
Esophagus
Crop
Hypopharyngeal gland
Brain
Hindgut
Rectum
Sting
Pharynx
Venom sac
Venom gland
Nerve ganglion
Salivary duct
Salivary gland
Ventriculus (midgut)
Ventral nerve cord
Proventriculus

EXTERNAL FEATURES OF AN ANT

Compound eye
Antenna
Foreleg
Mandible
Thorax
Head
Middle leg
Abdomen
Hind leg

EXTERNAL FEATURES OF A BEETLE

Flagellum
Claw
Tarsomere
Tarsus
Tibia
Pedicel
Femur
Trochanter
Mandible
Scape
Labrum
Coxa
Scutellum
Labial palp
Compound eye
Head
Prothorax
Mesothorax
Foreleg
Metathorax
Middle leg

Elytron
Costal margin
Apex
Vein
Wing
Abdomen
Hind leg

13

Arachnids

THE CLASS ARACHNIDA INCLUDES SPIDERS (order Araneae) and
scorpions (order Scorpiones). The class is part of the phylum
Arthropoda, which also includes insects and crustaceans.
Spiders and scorpions are characterized by having four pairs of
walking legs; a pair of pincer-like mouthparts called chelicerae; another
pair of frontal appendages called pedipalps, which are sensory in spiders
but used for grasping in scorpions; and a body divided into two
sections (a combined head and thorax called a cephalothorax
or prosoma, and an abdomen or opisthosoma).
Unlike other arthropods, spiders and
scorpions lack antennae. Spiders
and scorpions are carnivorous.
Spiders poison prey by biting
with the fanged chelicerae,
scorpions by stinging
with the end of the
metasoma (tail).

**MEXICAN TRUE RED-
LEGGED TARANTULA**
(Euathlus emilia)

INTERNAL ANATOMY OF A FEMALE SPIDER

Anterior aorta
Ostium
Pumping stomach
Heart
Digestive gland
Posterior aorta
Malpighian tubule
Brain
Intestine
Cloaca
Ovary
Simple eye
Anus
Poison gland
Spinneret
Poison duct
Chelicera
Silk gland
Fang
Oviduct
Trachea
Vagina
Book lung
Spermatheca (seminal receptacle)
Mouth
Gut cecum
Esophagus
Spiracle

EXTERNAL FEATURES OF A SCORPION

Chela (claw of pedipalp)
Pedipalp
Prosoma (cephalothorax)
Opisthosoma (abdomen)
Stinger
Metasoma (tail)
Chelicera
Median eye
Patella
Tibia
Tarsus
Femur
Coxa
3rd walking leg
4th walking leg
Claw
1st walking leg
Metatarsus
Trochanter
2nd walking leg

14

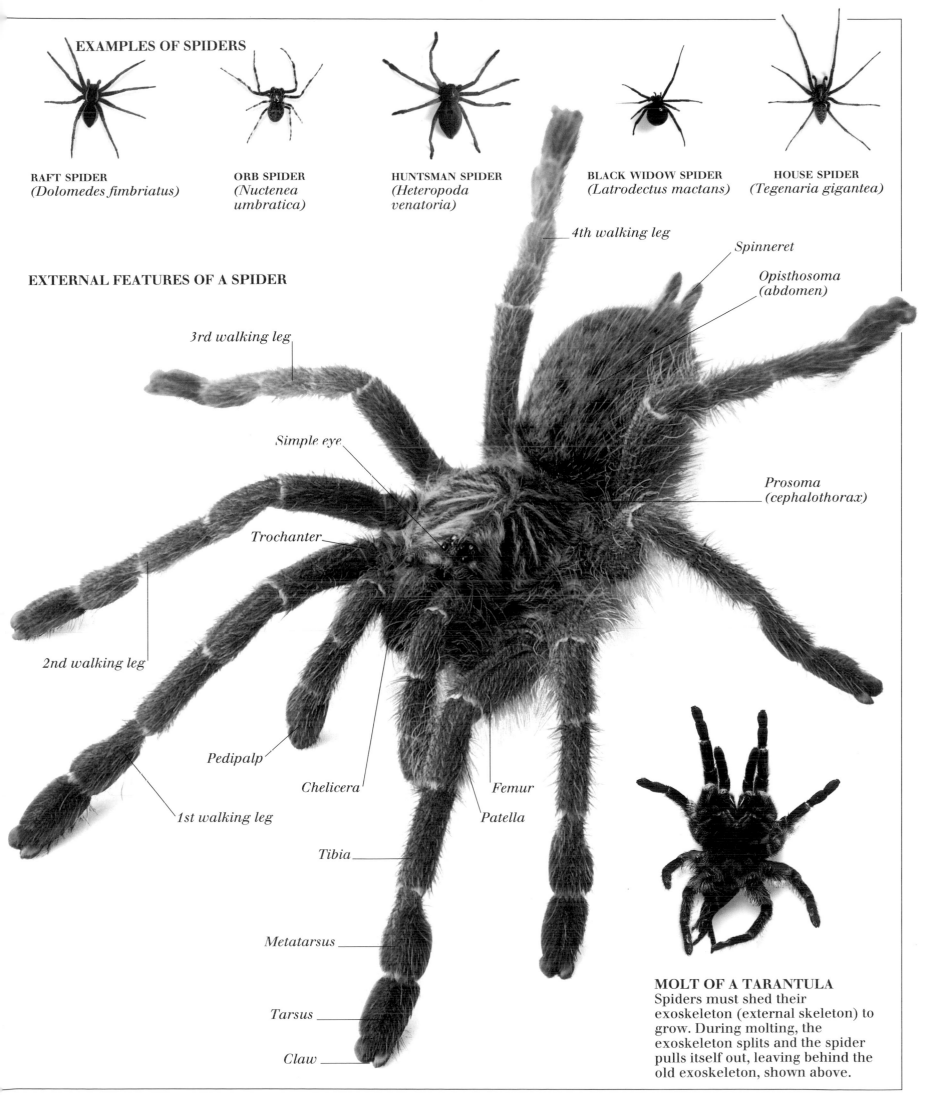

EXAMPLES OF SPIDERS

RAFT SPIDER
(Dolomedes fimbriatus)

ORB SPIDER
(Nuctenea umbratica)

HUNTSMAN SPIDER
(Heteropoda venatoria)

BLACK WIDOW SPIDER
(Latrodectus mactans)

HOUSE SPIDER
(Tegenaria gigantea)

EXTERNAL FEATURES OF A SPIDER

4th walking leg

Spinneret

Opisthosoma (abdomen)

3rd walking leg

Simple eye

Prosoma (cephalothorax)

Trochanter

2nd walking leg

Pedipalp

Chelicera

Femur

Patella

1st walking leg

Tibia

Metatarsus

Tarsus

Claw

MOLT OF A TARANTULA
Spiders must shed their exoskeleton (external skeleton) to grow. During molting, the exoskeleton splits and the spider pulls itself out, leaving behind the old exoskeleton, shown above.

Worms, flukes, and leeches

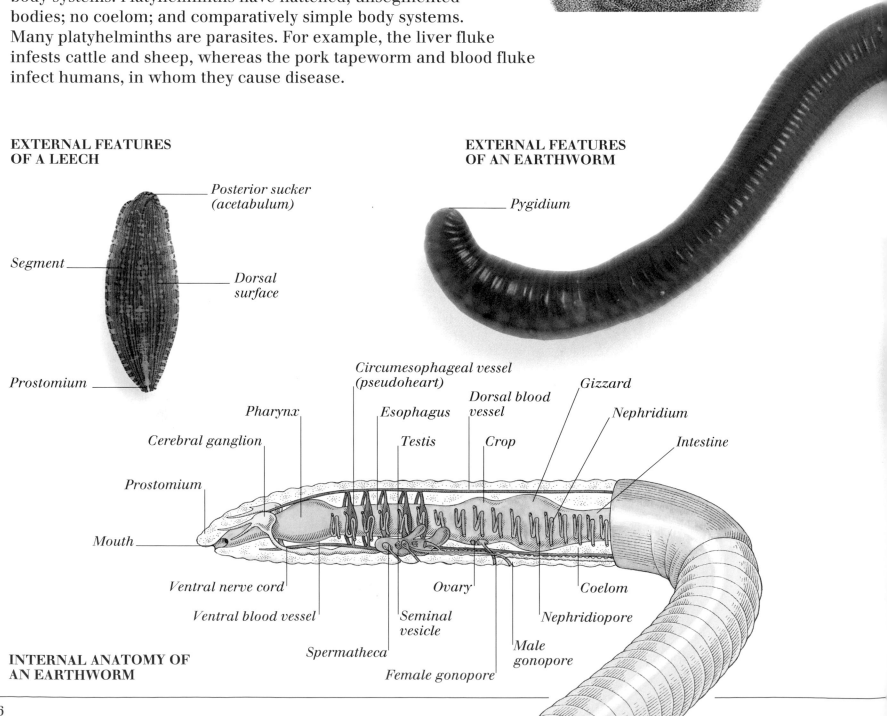

THE TERM "WORM" HAS NO STRICT SCIENTIFIC meaning, but it is commonly applied to various long, thin, soft-bodied animals. Probably the best-known groups of worms are the segmented worms (phylum Annelida), which include earthworms, marine worms such as sandworms and ragworms, and also leeches; and the flatworms (phylum Platyhelminthes), which include tapeworms and flukes. Annelid worms have cylindrical bodies divided into many segments; a coelom (body cavity) around the gut; and relatively well-developed nervous, circulatory, and other body systems. Platyhelminths have flattened, unsegmented bodies; no coelom; and comparatively simple body systems. Many platyhelminths are parasites. For example, the liver fluke infests cattle and sheep, whereas the pork tapeworm and blood fluke infect humans, in whom they cause disease.

HEAD (SCOLEX) OF A PORK TAPEWORM

Rostellum

Hook

Sucker (acetabulum

EXTERNAL FEATURES OF A LEECH

Posterior sucker (acetabulum)

Segment

Dorsal surface

Prostomium

EXTERNAL FEATURES OF AN EARTHWORM

Pygidium

Pharynx

Circumesophageal vessel (pseudoheart)

Esophagus

Dorsal blood vessel

Gizzard

Nephridium

Cerebral ganglion

Testis

Crop

Intestine

Prostomium

Mouth

Ventral nerve cord

Ovary

Coelom

Ventral blood vessel

Seminal vesicle

Nephridiopore

Spermatheca

Male gonopore

Female gonopore

INTERNAL ANATOMY OF AN EARTHWORM

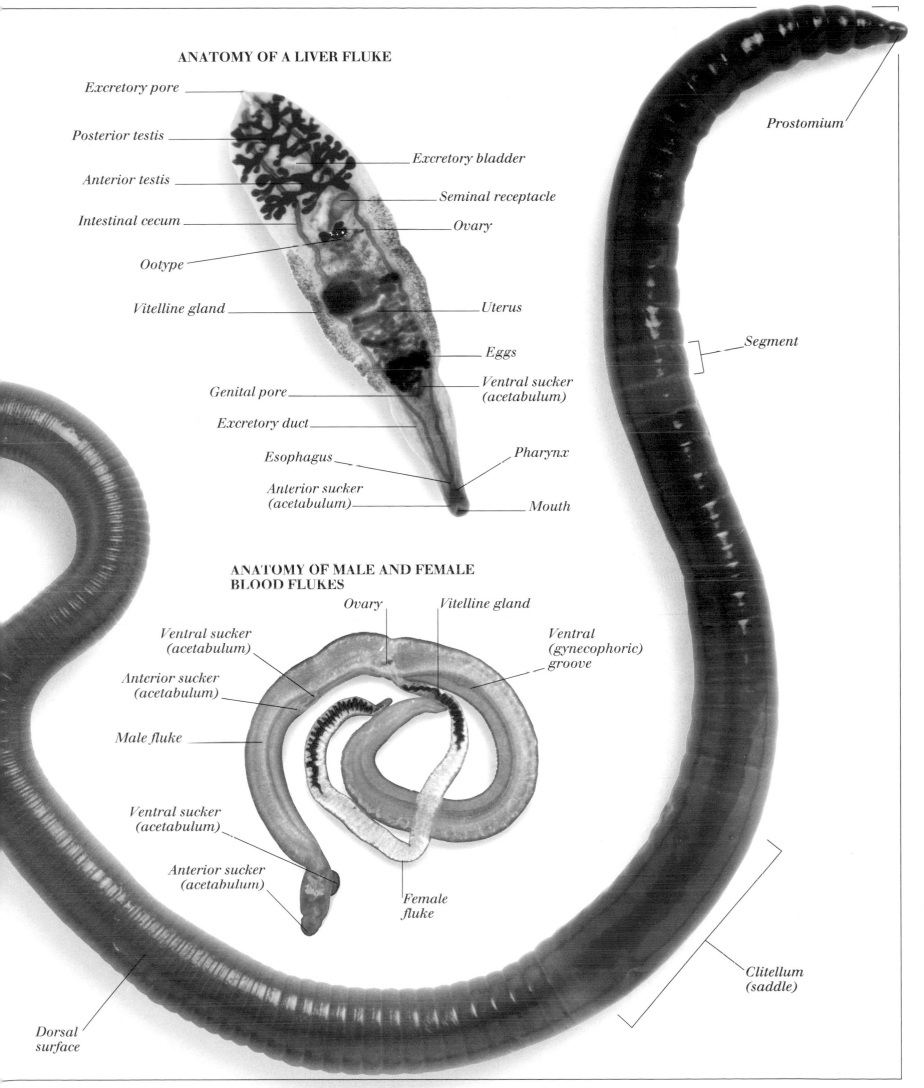

ANATOMY OF A LIVER FLUKE

Excretory pore

Posterior testis

Anterior testis

Intestinal cecum

Ootype

Vitelline gland

Genital pore

Excretory duct

Esophagus

Anterior sucker
(acetabulum)

Excretory bladder

Seminal receptacle

Ovary

Uterus

Eggs

Ventral sucker
(acetabulum)

Pharynx

Mouth

ANATOMY OF MALE AND FEMALE
BLOOD FLUKES

Ovary

Vitelline gland

Ventral sucker
(acetabulum)

Anterior sucker
(acetabulum)

Male fluke

Ventral
(gynecophoric)
groove

Ventral sucker
(acetabulum)

Anterior sucker
(acetabulum)

Female
fluke

Prostomium

Segment

Clitellum
(saddle)

Dorsal
surface

Sharks and jawless fish

SHARKS, DOGFISH (WHICH ARE actually small sharks), skates, and rays belong to a class of fishes called Chondrichthyes, which is a division of the superclass Gnathostomata (meaning "jawed mouths"). Also sometimes known as elasmobranchs, sharks and their relatives have a skeleton made of cartilage (hence their common name, cartilaginous fish), a characteristic that distinguishes them from bony fish (see pp. 20-21). Other important features of cartilaginous fish are extremely tough, tooth-like scales, and lack of a swim bladder. Jawless fish— lampreys and hagfish—are primitive, eel-like fish that make up the order Cyclostomata (meaning "round mouths"), a division of the superclass Agnatha (meaning "without jaws"). In addition to their characteristic round, sucker-like mouths and lack of jaws, cyclostomes also have smooth, slimy skin without scales, and unpaired fins.

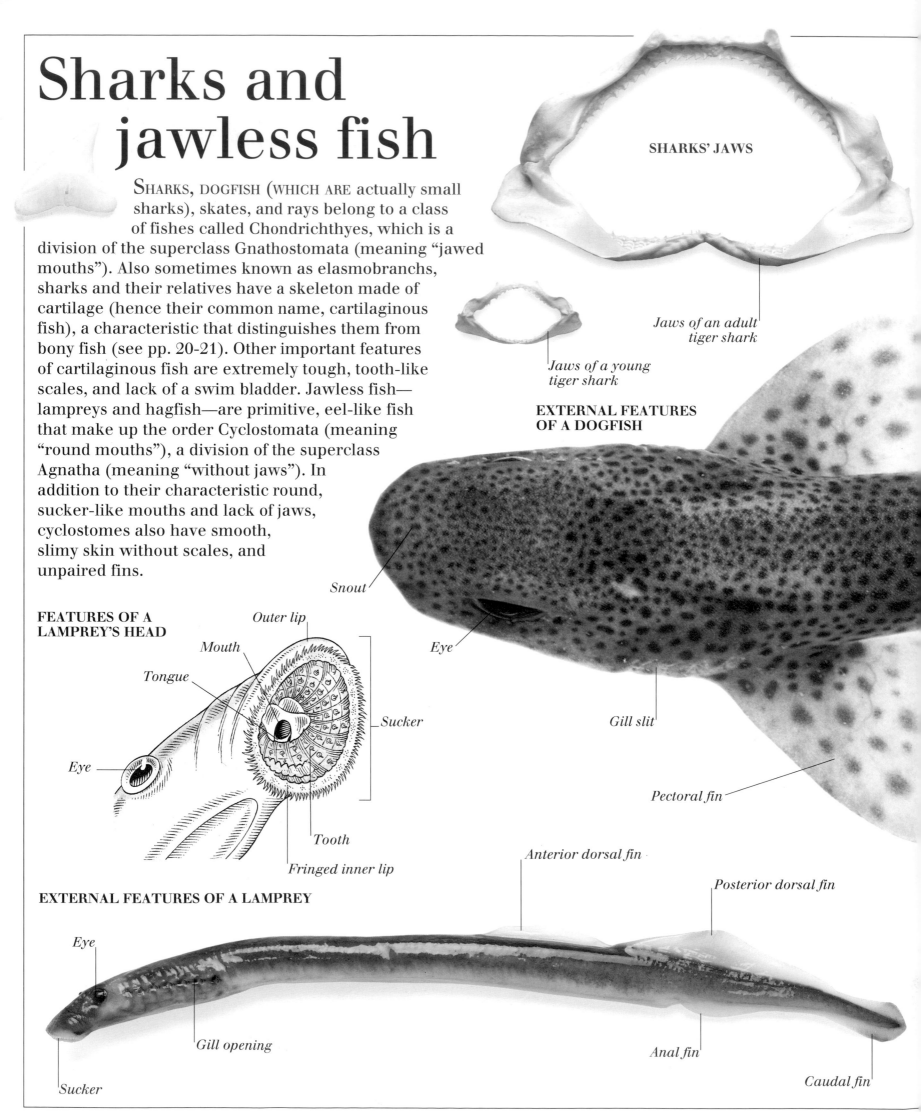

SHARKS' JAWS

Jaws of an adult tiger shark

Jaws of a young tiger shark

EXTERNAL FEATURES OF A DOGFISH

Snout

Eye

Gill slit

Pectoral fin

FEATURES OF A LAMPREY'S HEAD

Outer lip

Mouth

Tongue

Eye

Sucker

Tooth

Fringed inner lip

EXTERNAL FEATURES OF A LAMPREY

Eye

Gill opening

Sucker

Anterior dorsal fin

Posterior dorsal fin

Anal fin

Caudal fin

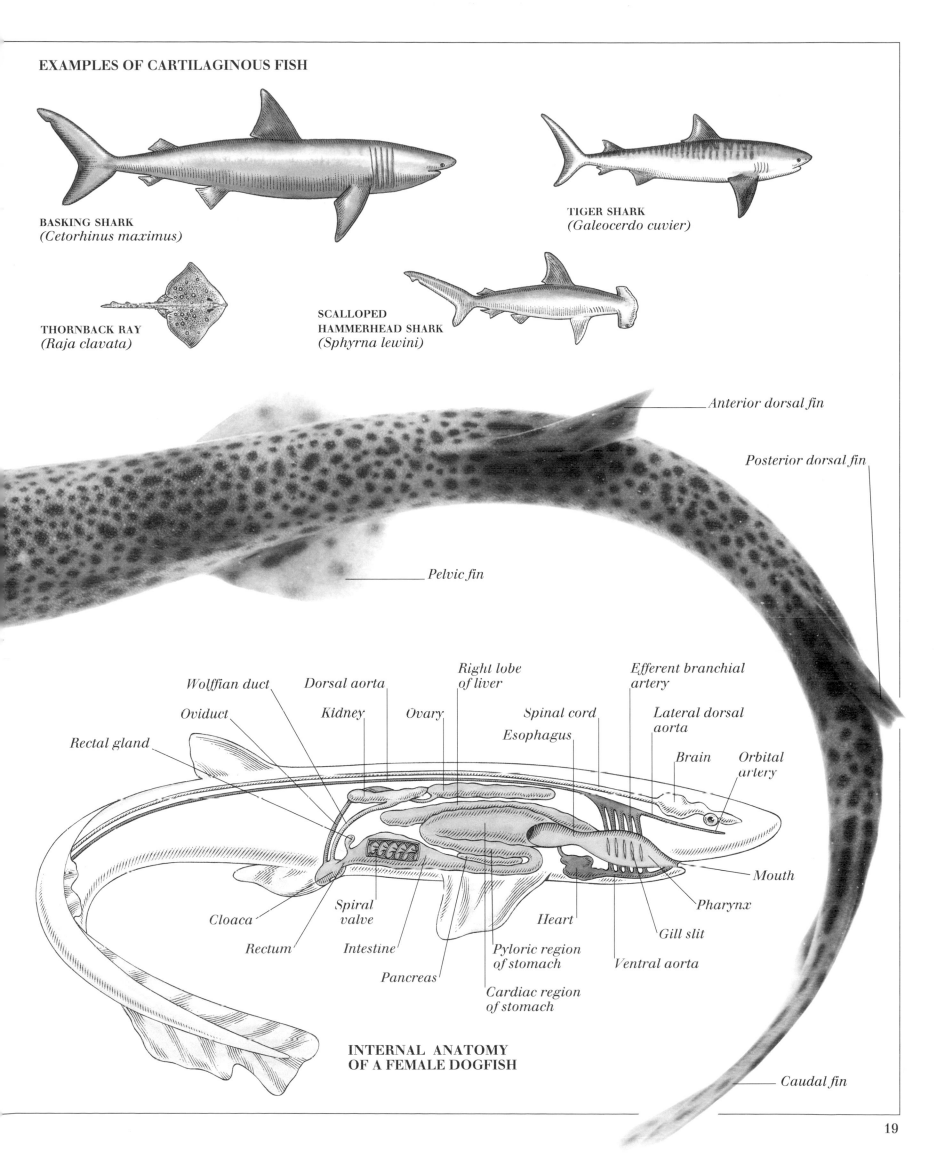

EXAMPLES OF CARTILAGINOUS FISH

BASKING SHARK
(*Cetorhinus maximus*)

TIGER SHARK
(*Galeocerdo cuvier*)

THORNBACK RAY
(*Raja clavata*)

**SCALLOPED
HAMMERHEAD SHARK**
(*Sphyrna lewini*)

Anterior dorsal fin

Posterior dorsal fin

Pelvic fin

Efferent branchial
artery

Right lobe
of liver

Spinal cord

Lateral dorsal
aorta

Wolffian duct

Dorsal aorta

Esophagus

Oviduct

Kidney

Ovary

Brain

Orbital
artery

Rectal gland

Mouth

Cloaca

Spiral
valve

Pharynx

Rectum

Intestine

Heart

Gill slit

Pyloric region
of stomach

Ventral aorta

Pancreas

Cardiac region
of stomach

**INTERNAL ANATOMY
OF A FEMALE DOGFISH**

Caudal fin

Bony fish

BONY FISH, SUCH AS CARP, TROUT, SALMON, perch, and cod, are by far the best known and largest group of fish, with more than 20,000 species (over 95 percent of all known fish). As their name suggests, bony fish have skeletons made of bone, in contrast to the cartilaginous skeletons of sharks, jawless fish, and their relatives (see pp. 18-19). Other typical features of bony fish include a swim bladder, which functions as a variable-buoyancy organ, enabling a fish to remain effortlessly at whatever depth it is swimming; relatively thin, bone-like scales; a flap (called an operculum) covering the gills; and paired pelvic and pectoral fins. Scientifically, bony fish belong to the class Osteichthyes, which is a division of the superclass Gnathostomata (meaning "jawed mouths").

HOW FISH BREATHE

Fish "breathe" by extracting oxygen from water through their gills. Water is sucked in through the mouth; simultaneously, the opercula close to prevent the water from escaping. The mouth is then closed, and muscles in the walls of the mouth, pharynx, and opercular cavity contract to pump the water inside over the gills and out through the opercula. Some fish rely on swimming with their mouths open to keep water flowing over the gills.

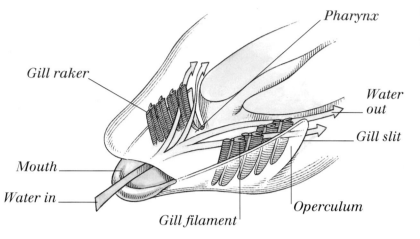

Pharynx

Gill raker

Water out

Gill slit

Mouth

Operculum

Water in

Gill filament

EXAMPLES OF BONY FISH

MANDARINFISH
(Synchiropus splendidus)

ANGLERFISH
(Caulophryne jordani)

OCEANIC SEAHORSE
(Hippocampus kuda)

LIONFISH
(Pterois volitans)

Vertebra

Neural spine

Hypural

Hemal spine

Caudal fin ray

Radial cartilage

Anal fin ray

STURGEON
(Acipenser sturio)

SNOWFLAKE MORAY EEL
(Echidna nebulosa)

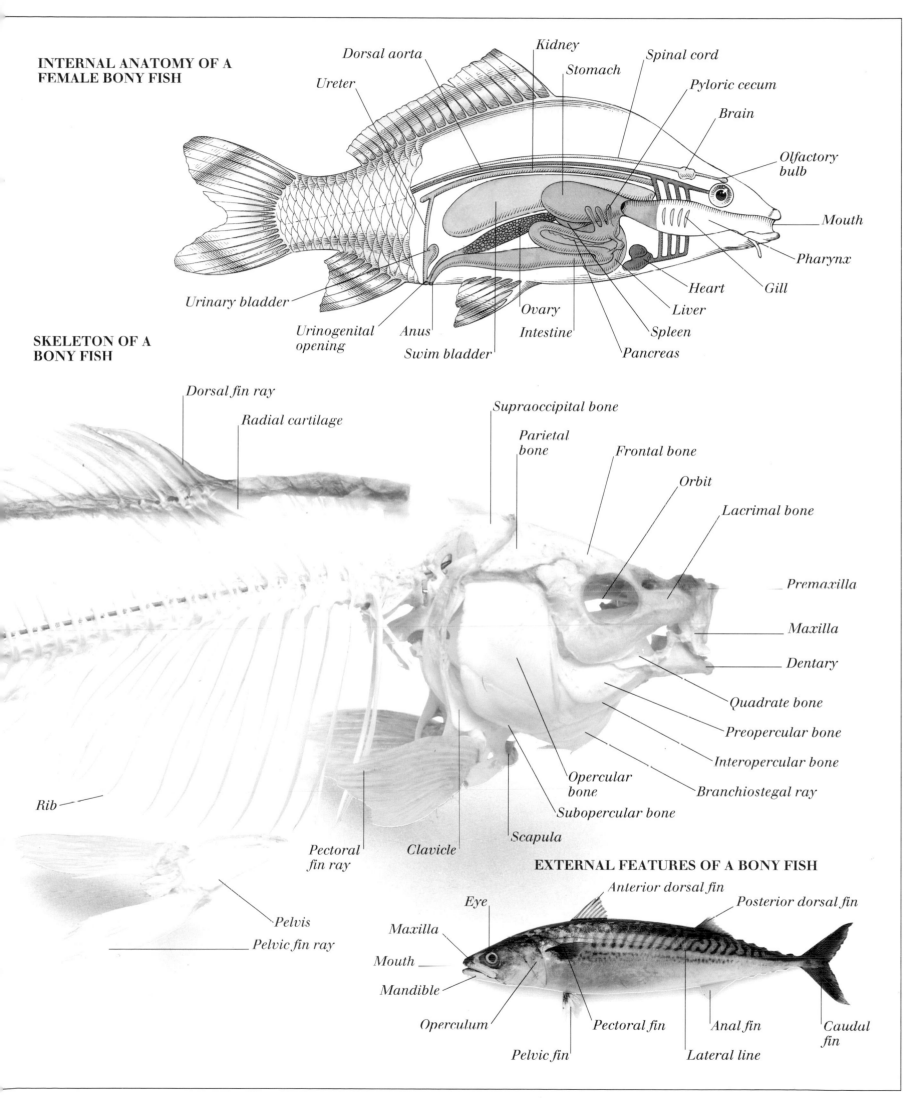

INTERNAL ANATOMY OF A FEMALE BONY FISH

Dorsal aorta
Kidney
Ureter
Stomach
Spinal cord
Pyloric cecum
Brain
Olfactory bulb
Mouth
Pharynx
Heart
Gill
Urinary bladder
Liver
Urinogenital opening
Anus
Ovary
Intestine
Spleen
Swim bladder
Pancreas

SKELETON OF A BONY FISH

Dorsal fin ray
Radial cartilage
Supraoccipital bone
Parietal bone
Frontal bone
Orbit
Lacrimal bone
Premaxilla
Maxilla
Dentary
Quadrate bone
Preopercular bone
Interopercular bone
Branchiostegal ray
Opercular bone
Subopercular bone
Scapula
Rib
Pectoral fin ray
Clavicle
Pelvis
Pelvic fin ray

EXTERNAL FEATURES OF A BONY FISH

Anterior dorsal fin
Posterior dorsal fin
Eye
Maxilla
Mouth
Mandible
Operculum
Pelvic fin
Pectoral fin
Anal fin
Lateral line
Caudal fin

21

Starfish and sea urchins

STARFISH, SEA URCHINS, AND THEIR relatives (including feather stars, brittle stars, basket stars, sea daisies, sea lilies, and sea cucumbers) make up the phylum Echinodermata. A unique feature of echinoderms is the water vascular system, which consists of a series of water-filled canals from which protrude thousands of tiny tube feet. The tube feet may be used for movement, feeding, or respiration. Other features include pentaradiate symmetry (that is, the body can be divided into five parts radiating from the center); no head; a diffuse, decentralized nervous system that lacks a brain; and no excretory organs. Typically, echinoderms also have an endoskeleton (internal skeleton) consisting of hard calcite ossicles embedded in the body wall and often bearing protruding spines or tubercles. The ossicles may fit together to form a test (as in sea urchins) or remain separate (as in sea cucumbers).

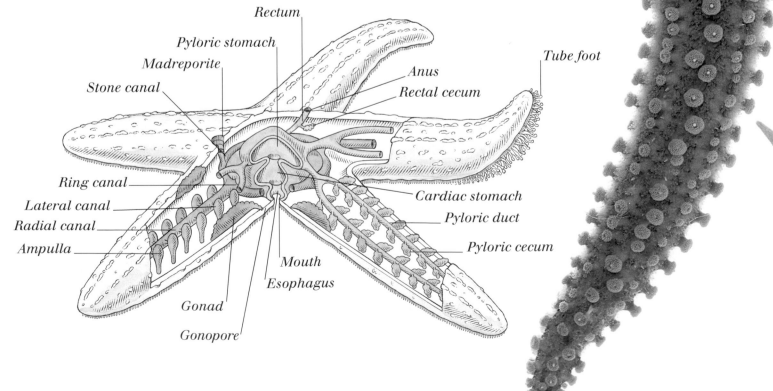

EXTERNAL FEATURES OF A STARFISH (UPPER, OR ABORAL, SURFACE)

Disk

Madreporite

Spine

Arm

INTERNAL ANATOMY OF A STARFISH

Rectum

Pyloric stomach

Madreporite

Stone canal

Anus

Rectal cecum

Tube foot

Ring canal

Cardiac stomach

Lateral canal

Pyloric duct

Radial canal

Pyloric cecum

Ampulla

Mouth

Esophagus

Gonad

Gonopore

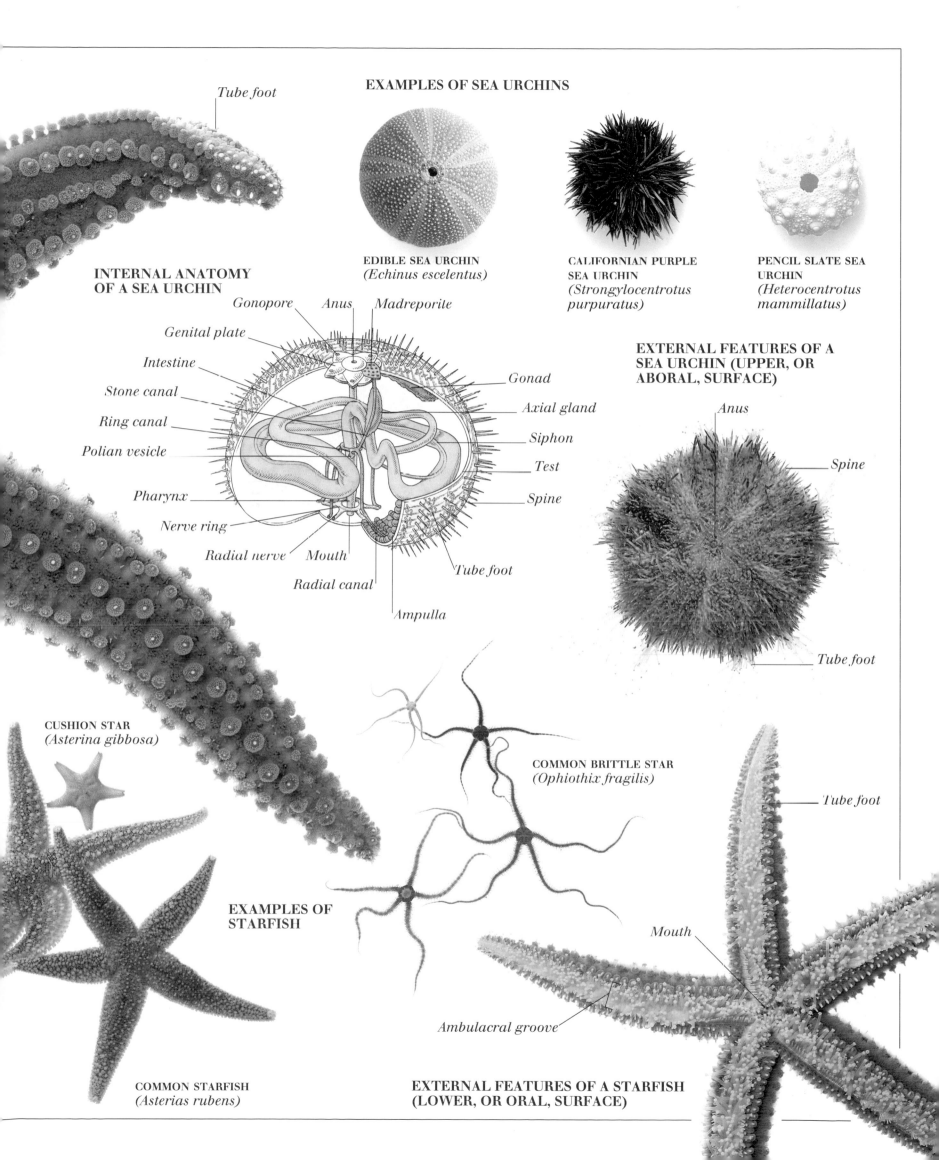

Tube foot

EXAMPLES OF SEA URCHINS

EDIBLE SEA URCHIN
(Echinus escelentus)

**CALIFORNIAN PURPLE
SEA URCHIN
(Strongylocentrotus
purpuratus)**

**PENCIL SLATE SEA
URCHIN
(Heterocentrotus
mammillatus)**

INTERNAL ANATOMY
OF A SEA URCHIN

Gonopore   *Anus*   *Madreporite*

Genital plate

Intestine

Stone canal

Ring canal

Polian vesicle

Pharynx

Nerve ring

Radial nerve   *Mouth*

Radial canal

Ampulla

Gonad

Axial gland

Siphon

Test

Spine

Tube foot

EXTERNAL FEATURES OF A
SEA URCHIN (UPPER, OR
ABORAL, SURFACE)

Anus

Spine

Tube foot

CUSHION STAR
(Asterina gibbosa)

COMMON BRITTLE STAR
(Ophiothix fragilis)

Tube foot

EXAMPLES OF
STARFISH

Mouth

Ambulacral groove

COMMON STARFISH
(Asterias rubens)

EXTERNAL FEATURES OF A STARFISH
(LOWER, OR ORAL, SURFACE)

Sponges, jellyfish, and sea anemones

SPONGES ARE MAINLY MARINE animals that make up the phylum Porifera. They are among the simplest of all animals, having no tissues or organs. Their bodies consist of two layers of cells separated by a jelly-like layer (mesohyal) that is strengthened by mineral spicules or protein fibers. The body is perforated by a system of pores and water channels called the aquiferous system. Special cells (choanocytes) with whip-like structures (flagella) draw water through the aquiferous system, thereby bringing tiny food particles to the sponge's cells. Jellyfish (class Scyphozoa), sea anemones (class Anthozoa), and corals (also class Anthozoa) belong to the phylum Cnidaria, also known as Coelenterata. More complex than sponges, coelenterates have simple tissues, such as nervous tissue; a radially symmetrical body; and a mouth surrounded by tentacles with unique stinging cells (cnidocytes).

Amebocyte

Osculum (excurrent pore)

Choanocyte (collar cell)

Ostium (incurrent pore)

Porocyte (pore cell)

Mesohyal

Spongocoel (atrium; paragaster)

Spicule

Pinacocyte (epidermal cell)

Ostium (incurrent pore)

SKELETON OF A SPONGE

EXTERNAL FEATURES OF A SEA ANEMONE

Protein matrix

Pore

Tentacle

EXAMPLES OF SEA ANEMONES

JEWEL ANEMONE
(Corynactis viridis)

PARASITIC ANEMONE
(Calliactis parasitica)

PLUMOSE ANEMONE
(Metridium senile)

MEDITERRANEAN SEA ANEMONE
(Condylactis sp.)

GREEN SNAKELOCK ANEMONE
(Anemonia viridis)

BEADLET ANEMONE
(Actinia equina)

GHOST ANEMONE
(Actinothoe sphyrodeta)

Sagartia elegans

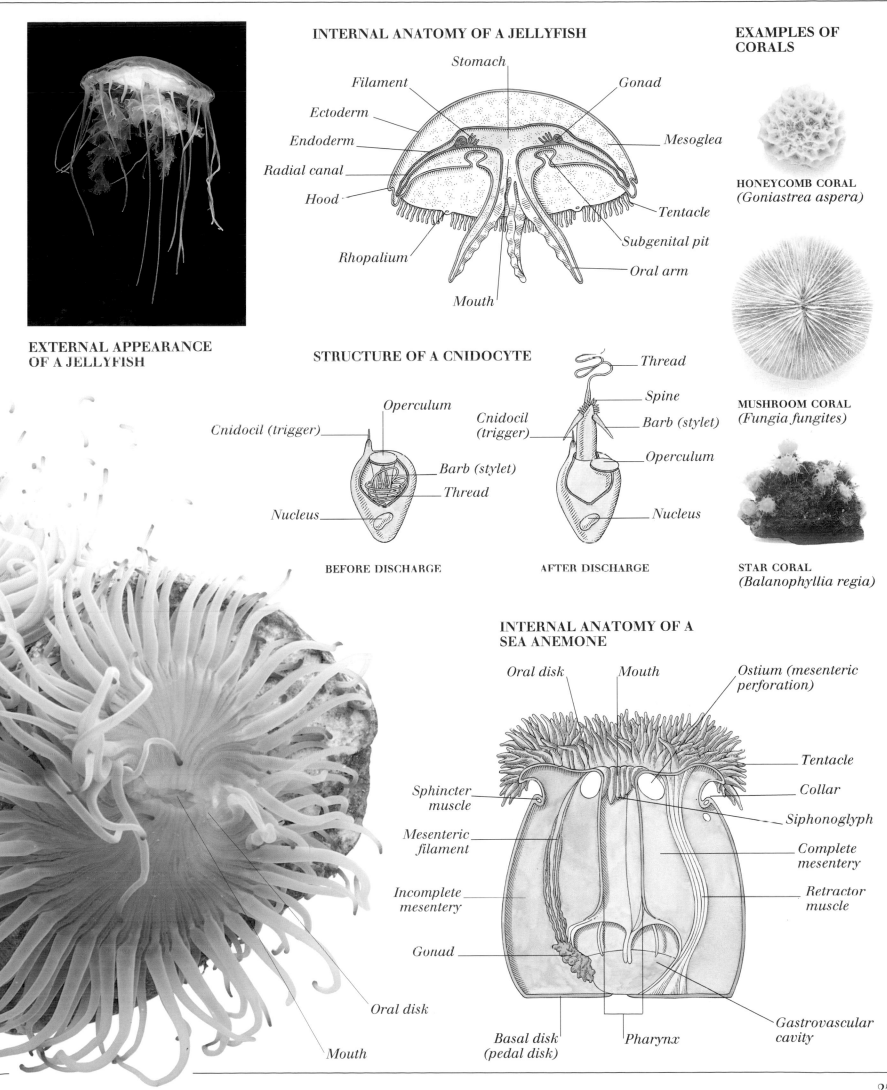

INTERNAL ANATOMY OF A JELLYFISH

Stomach

Filament

Gonad

Ectoderm

Endoderm

Mesoglea

Radial canal

Hood

Tentacle

Rhopalium

Subgenital pit

Oral arm

Mouth

**EXTERNAL APPEARANCE
OF A JELLYFISH**

**EXAMPLES OF
CORALS**

HONEYCOMB CORAL
(Goniastrea aspera)

MUSHROOM CORAL
(Fungia fungites)

STAR CORAL
(Balanophyllia regia)

STRUCTURE OF A CNIDOCYTE

Operculum

Thread

Cnidocil (trigger)

Spine

Cnidocil
(trigger)

Barb (stylet)

Barb (stylet)

Operculum

Thread

Nucleus

Nucleus

BEFORE DISCHARGE

AFTER DISCHARGE

**INTERNAL ANATOMY OF A
SEA ANEMONE**

Oral disk

Mouth

Ostium (mesenteric
perforation)

Tentacle

Sphincter
muscle

Collar

Siphonoglyph

Mesenteric
filament

Complete
mesentery

Incomplete
mesentery

Retractor
muscle

Gonad

Oral disk

Gastrovascular
cavity

Mouth

Basal disk
(pedal disk)

Pharynx

Mollusks

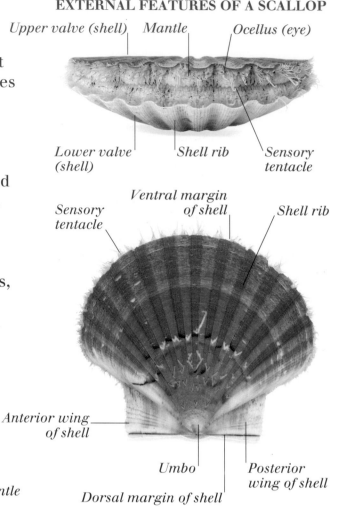

Upper valve (shell)   *Mantle*   *Ocellus (eye)*

Lower valve (shell)   *Shell rib*   *Sensory tentacle*

Sensory tentacle   *Ventral margin of shell*   *Shell rib*

Anterior wing of shell

Umbo   *Posterior wing of shell*

Dorsal margin of shell

THE PHYLUM MOLLUSCA (MOLLUSKS) is a large group of animals that includes octopuses, snails, and scallops. Octopuses and their relatives —including squid and cuttlefish—form the class Cephalopoda. Cephalopods typically have a head with a radula (a file-like feeding organ) and beak; a well-developed nervous system; sucker-bearing tentacles; a muscular mantle (part of the body wall) that can expel water through the siphon, enabling movement by jet propulsion; and a small shell or no shell. Snails and their relatives—including slugs, limpets, and abalones—make up the class Gastropoda. Gastropods typically have a coiled external shell, although some, such as slugs, have a small internal shell or no shell; a flat foot; and a head with tentacles and a radula. Scallops and their relatives—including clams, mussels, and oysters—make up the class Bivalvia (also called Pelecypoda). Features of bivalves include a shell with two halves (valves); large gills that are used for breathing and filter feeding; and no radula.

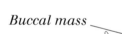

INTERNAL ANATOMY OF AN OCTOPUS

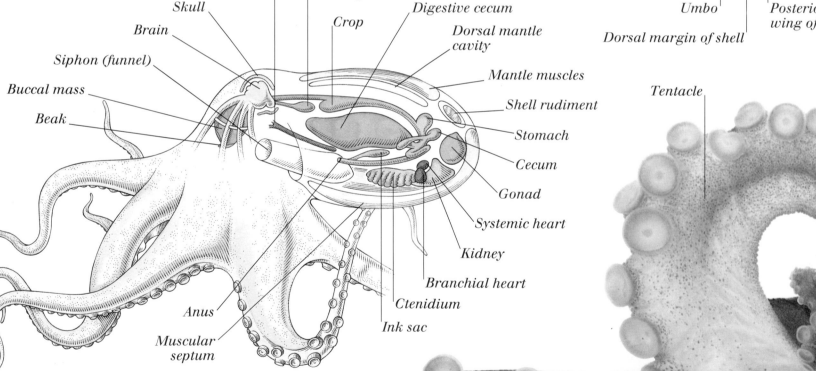

Cephalic vein   *Poison gland*   *Digestive cecum*

Skull   *Crop*   *Dorsal mantle cavity*

Brain   *Mantle muscles*

Siphon (funnel)   *Shell rudiment*

Buccal mass   *Stomach*

Beak   *Cecum*

Gonad

Systemic heart

Kidney

Branchial heart

Anus

Ctenidium

Muscular septum   *Ink sac*

Tentacle

Sucker

26

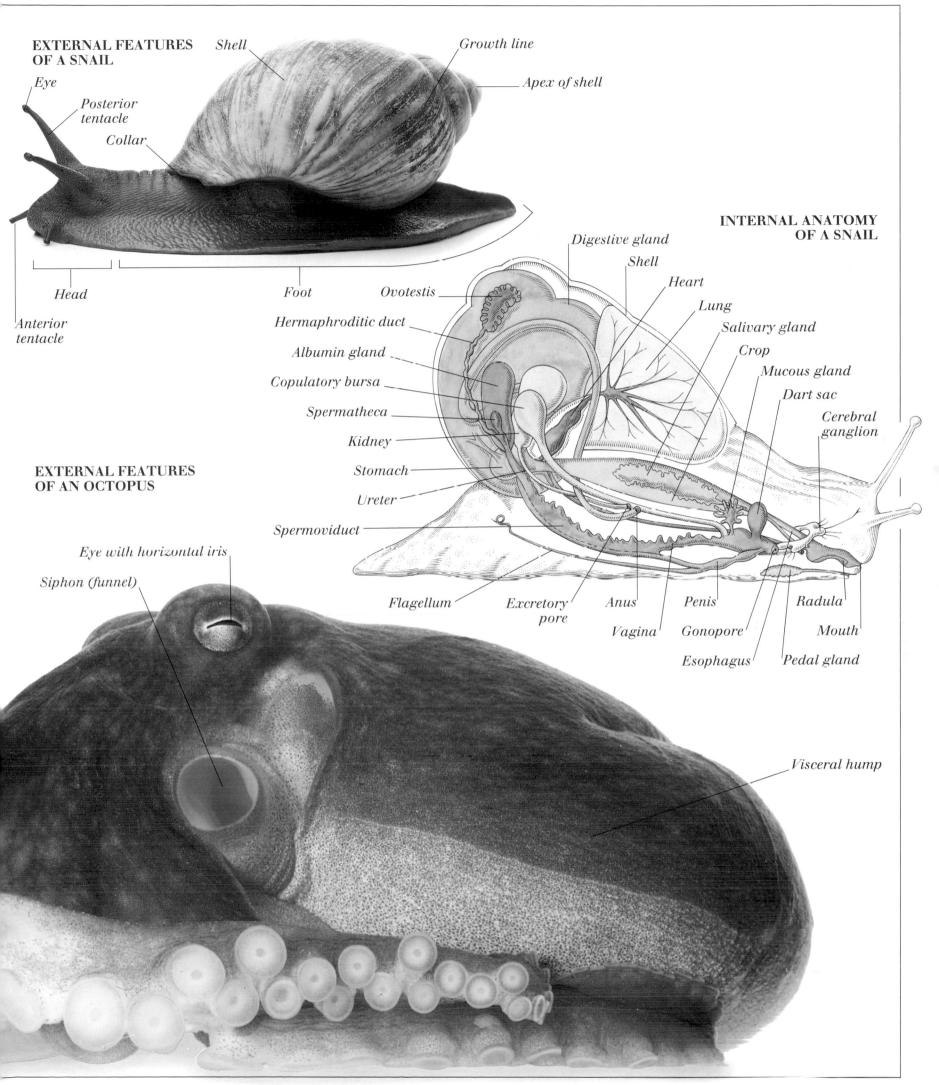

EXTERNAL FEATURES OF A SNAIL

Eye

Posterior tentacle

Collar

Shell

Growth line

Apex of shell

Anterior tentacle

Head

Foot

INTERNAL ANATOMY OF A SNAIL

Digestive gland

Shell

Heart

Lung

Salivary gland

Crop

Mucous gland

Dart sac

Cerebral ganglion

Ovotestis

Hermaphroditic duct

Albumin gland

Copulatory bursa

Spermatheca

Kidney

Stomach

Ureter

Spermoviduct

Flagellum

Excretory pore

Anus

Vagina

Penis

Gonopore

Esophagus

Radula

Mouth

Pedal gland

EXTERNAL FEATURES OF AN OCTOPUS

Eye with horizontal iris

Siphon (funnel)

Visceral hump

27

Crustaceans

THE SUBPHYLUM CRUSTACEA is one of the largest groups in the phylum Arthropoda. The subphylum is divided into several classes, the most important of which are Malacostraca and Cirripedia. The class Malacostraca includes crayfish, crabs, lobsters, and shrimps. Typical features of malacostracans include a body divided into two sections (a combined head and thorax called a cephalothorax, and an abdomen); an exoskeleton (external skeleton) with a large plate (carapace) covering the cephalothorax; stalked, compound eyes; and two pairs of antennae. The class Cirripedia includes barnacles, which, unlike other crustaceans, spend their adult lives attached to a surface, such as a rock. Other characteristics of cirripedes include an exoskeleton of overlapping calcareous plates; a body consisting almost entirely of thorax (the abdomen and head are minute); and six pairs of thoracic appendages (cirri) used for filter feeding.

1st swimmeret (1st pleopod)

2nd swimmeret (2nd pleopod)

3rd swimmeret (3rd pleopod)

4th swimmeret (4th pleopod)

5th swimmeret (5th pleopod)

Telson

Abdomen

Endopod
Exopod
Uropod

Abdominal segment

3rd leg (3rd pereopod)

5th leg (5th pereopod)

4th leg (4th pereopod)

2nd leg (2nd pereopod)

EXTERNAL FEATURES OF A CRAB

Propodus

Carpus

Dactylus

Compound eye

Antenna

Cheliped (chela; claw; 1st leg; 1st pereopod)

Carapace (shell)

Merus

Abdomen

2nd leg (2nd pereopod)

5th leg (5th pereopod)

3rd leg (3rd pereopod)

4th leg (4th pereopod)

EXTERNAL FEATURES OF A SHRIMP

Cephalothorax

Compound eye

Abdomen

Antenna

Leg (pereopod)

Swimmeret (pleopod)

Uropod
Exopod
Endopod

Telson

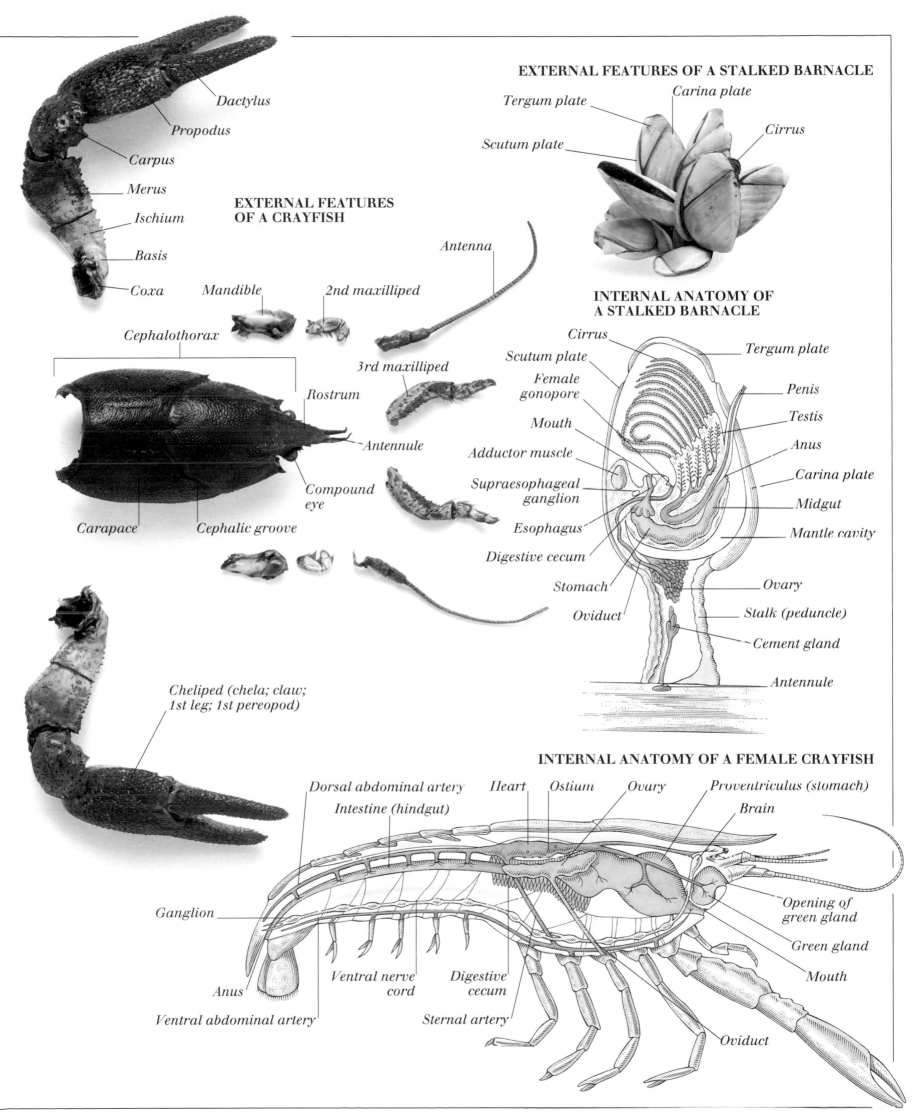

EXTERNAL FEATURES OF A STALKED BARNACLE

Tergum plate
Carina plate
Scutum plate
Cirrus

Dactylus
Propodus
Carpus
Merus
Ischium
Basis
Coxa

EXTERNAL FEATURES OF A CRAYFISH

Mandible
2nd maxilliped
Antenna

Cephalothorax
Rostrum
3rd maxilliped

Antennule
Compound eye

Carapace
Cephalic groove

INTERNAL ANATOMY OF A STALKED BARNACLE

Cirrus
Tergum plate
Scutum plate
Penis
Female gonopore
Testis
Mouth
Anus
Adductor muscle
Carina plate
Supraesophageal ganglion
Midgut
Esophagus
Mantle cavity
Digestive cecum
Stomach
Ovary
Oviduct
Stalk (peduncle)
Cement gland
Antennule

Cheliped (chela; claw; 1st leg; 1st pereopod)

INTERNAL ANATOMY OF A FEMALE CRAYFISH

Dorsal abdominal artery
Heart
Ostium
Ovary
Proventriculus (stomach)
Intestine (hindgut)
Brain

Ganglion
Opening of green gland
Green gland
Mouth

Anus
Ventral nerve cord
Digestive cecum
Sternal artery
Oviduct
Ventral abdominal artery

Amphibians

THE CLASS AMPHIBIA INCLUDES FROGS and toads (which make up the order Anura) and newts and salamanders (which make up the order Urodela). Amphibians typically have moist, scaleless, hairless skin; lungs; and are cold-blooded. They also undergo complete metamorphosis, from eggs laid in water through various water-living larval stages (such as the tadpole stage) to land-living adults. Typical features of adult frogs and toads include a squat body with no tail; long, powerful hind legs; and large, often bulging, eyes. Adult newts and salamanders typically have a long body with a well-developed tail; and relatively short legs of equal size. However, newts and salamanders show considerable variation; for example, in some species the adults have minute legs, external gills rather than lungs, and spend their entire lives in water.

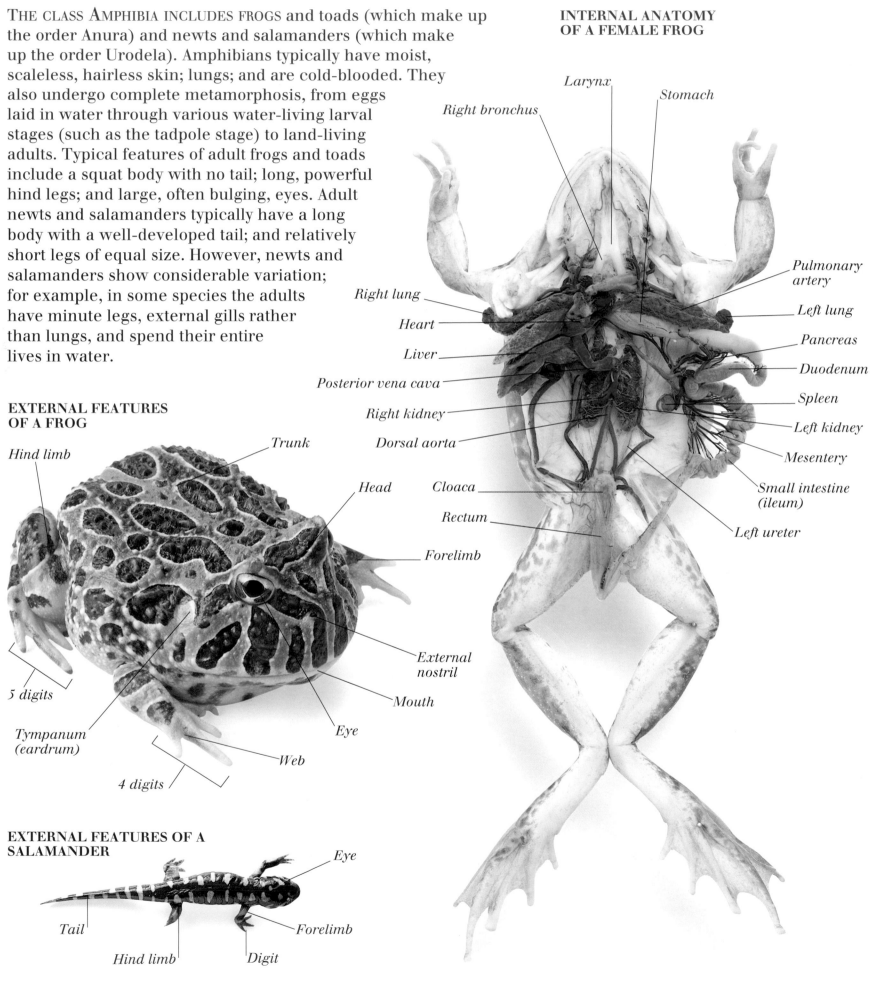

INTERNAL ANATOMY OF A FEMALE FROG

Larynx

Right bronchus

Stomach

Pulmonary artery

Right lung

Heart

Left lung

Liver

Pancreas

Posterior vena cava

Duodenum

Right kidney

Spleen

Dorsal aorta

Left kidney

Cloaca

Mesentery

Rectum

Small intestine (ileum)

Left ureter

EXTERNAL FEATURES OF A FROG

Hind limb

Trunk

Head

Forelimb

5 digits

External nostril

Tympanum (eardrum)

Mouth

Web

Eye

4 digits

EXTERNAL FEATURES OF A SALAMANDER

Eye

Tail

Forelimb

Hind limb

Digit

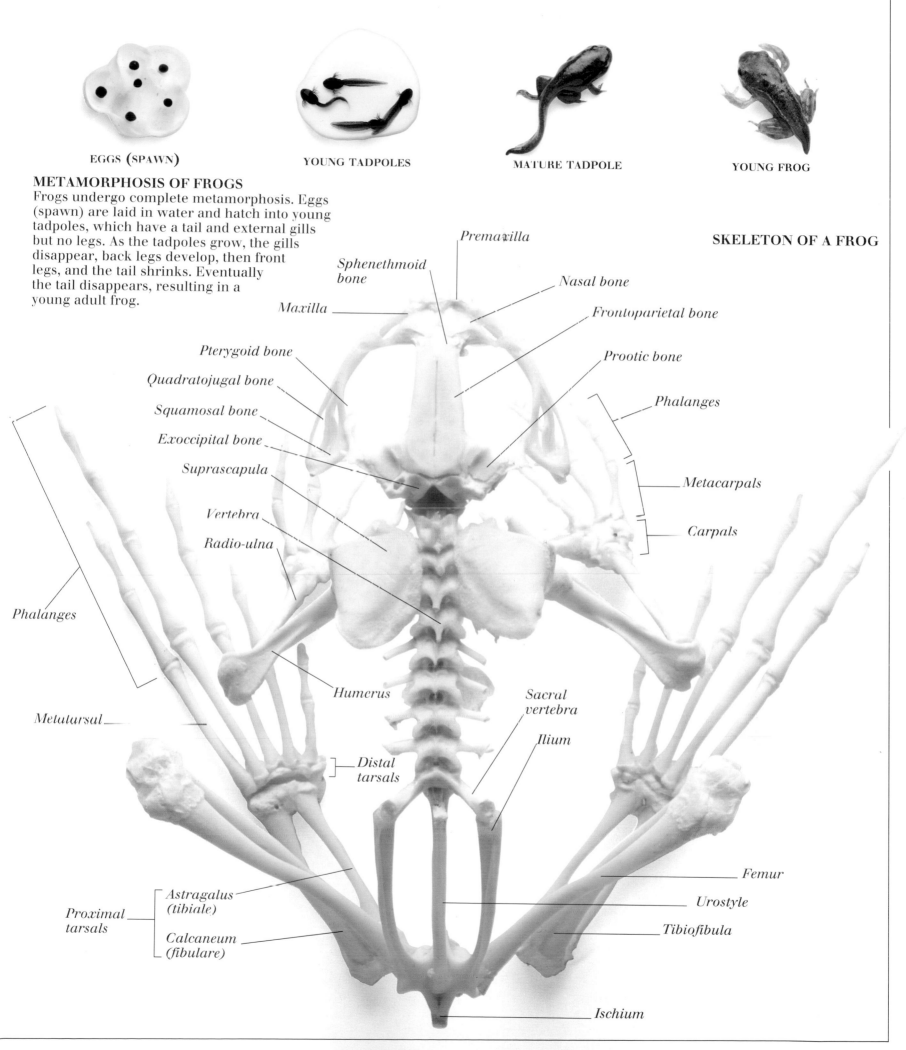

EGGS (SPAWN)

YOUNG TADPOLES

MATURE TADPOLE

YOUNG FROG

METAMORPHOSIS OF FROGS

Frogs undergo complete metamorphosis. Eggs (spawn) are laid in water and hatch into young tadpoles, which have a tail and external gills but no legs. As the tadpoles grow, the gills disappear, back legs develop, then front legs, and the tail shrinks. Eventually the tail disappears, resulting in a young adult frog.

SKELETON OF A FROG

Premaxilla

Sphenethmoid bone

Nasal bone

Maxilla

Frontoparietal bone

Pterygoid bone

Prootic bone

Quadratojugal bone

Phalanges

Squamosal bone

Exoccipital bone

Metacarpals

Suprascapula

Carpals

Vertebra

Radio-ulna

Phalanges

Humerus

Sacral vertebra

Metatarsal

Ilium

Distal tarsals

Proximal tarsals

Astragalus (tibiale)

Femur

Urostyle

Calcaneum (fibulare)

Tibiofibula

Ischium

Lizards and snakes

LIZARDS AND SNAKES BELONG to the order Squamata, a division of the class Reptilia. Characteristic reptilian features include scaly skin, lungs, and cold-bloodedness. Most reptiles lay leathery-shelled eggs, although some hatch the eggs inside their bodies and give birth to live young. Lizards belong to the suborder Lacertilia. Typically, they have long tails, and shed their skin in several pieces. Many lizards can regenerate a tail if it is lost; some can change color; and some are limbless. Snakes make up the suborder Ophidia (also called Serpentes). All snakes have long, limbless bodies; can dislocate their lower jaw to swallow large prey; and have eyelids that are joined together to form a single transparent covering over the front of the eye. Most snakes shed their skin in a single piece. Constrictor snakes kill their prey by squeezing; venomous snakes poison their prey.

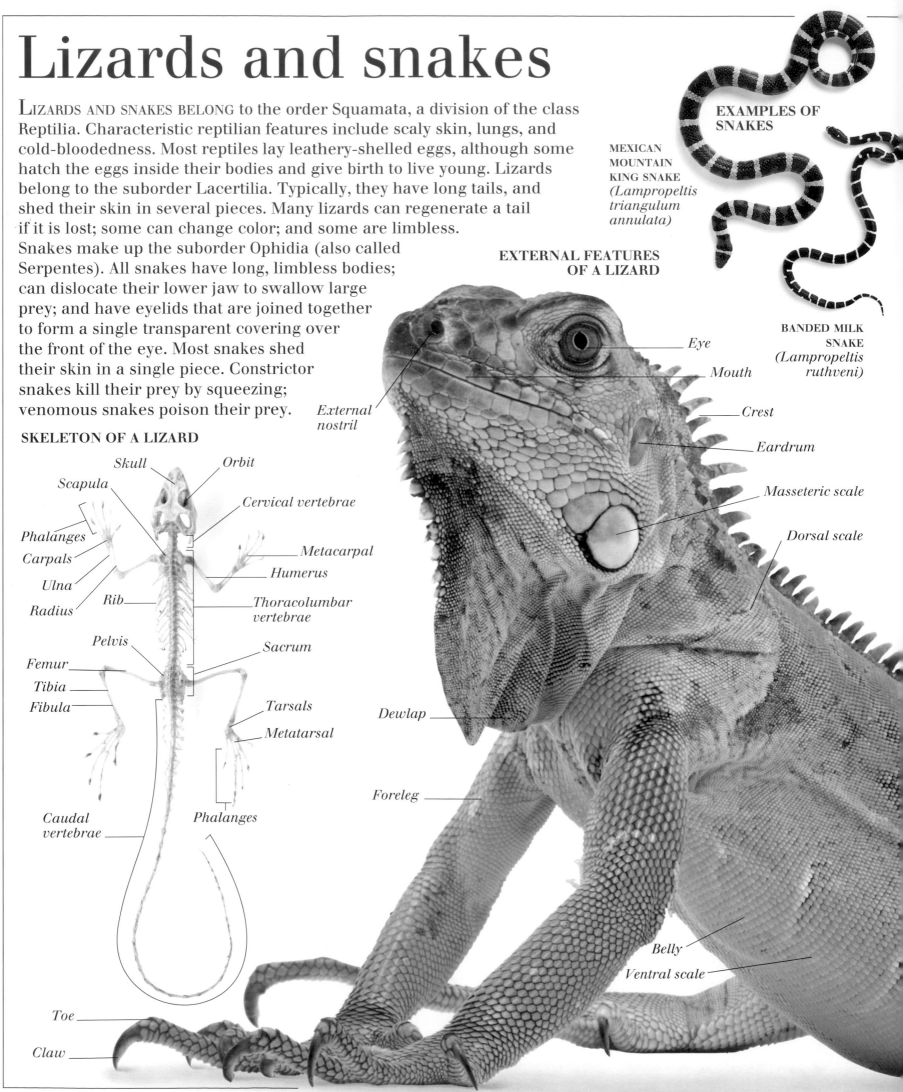

EXAMPLES OF SNAKES

MEXICAN MOUNTAIN KING SNAKE
(*Lampropeltis triangulum annulata*)

BANDED MILK SNAKE
(*Lampropeltis ruthveni*)

EXTERNAL FEATURES OF A LIZARD

Eye

Mouth

Crest

Eardrum

Masseteric scale

Dorsal scale

Dewlap

Foreleg

Belly

Ventral scale

External nostril

SKELETON OF A LIZARD

Skull

Orbit

Scapula

Cervical vertebrae

Phalanges

Carpals

Metacarpal

Humerus

Ulna

Radius

Rib

Thoracolumbar vertebrae

Pelvis

Sacrum

Femur

Tibia

Fibula

Tarsals

Metatarsal

Caudal vertebrae

Phalanges

Toe

Claw

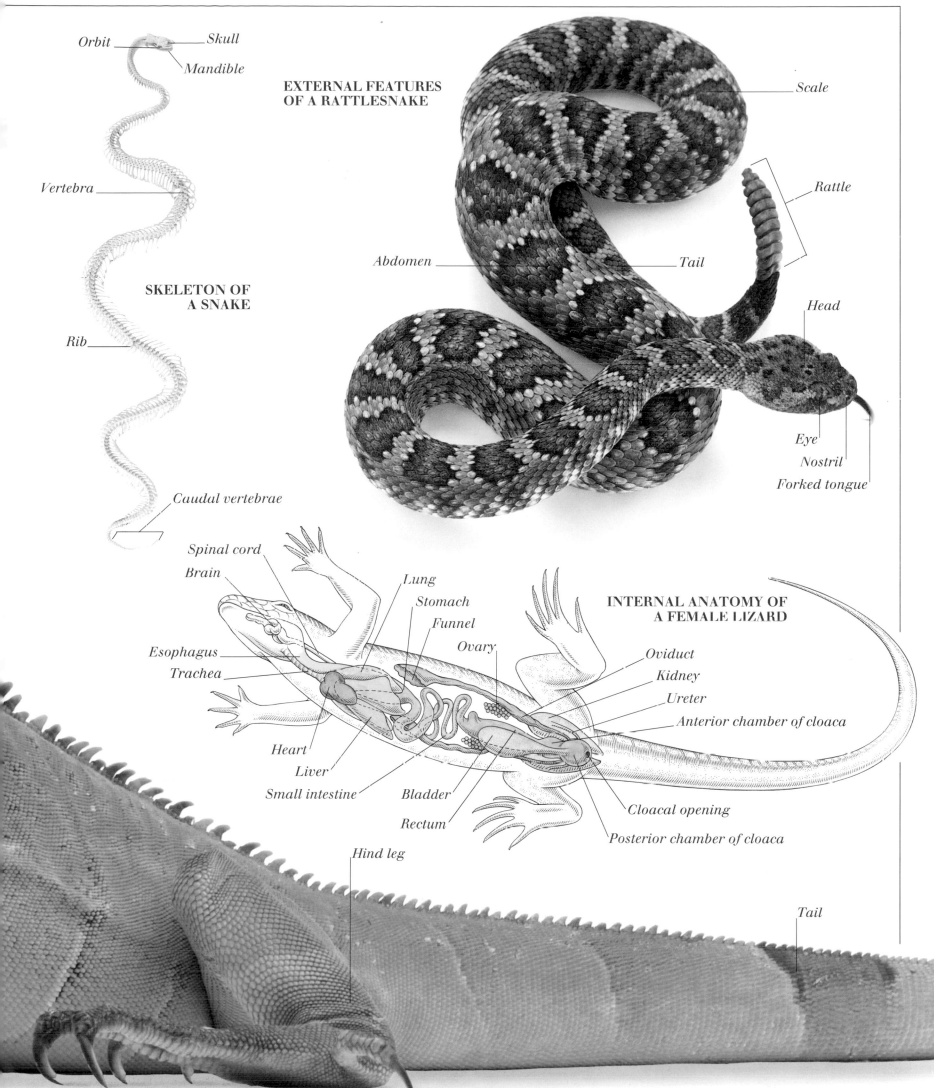

Orbit — Skull

Mandible

EXTERNAL FEATURES OF A RATTLESNAKE

Scale

Vertebra

Rattle

SKELETON OF A SNAKE

Rib

Abdomen — Tail

Head

Caudal vertebrae

Eye

Nostril

Forked tongue

Spinal cord

Brain

Lung

Stomach

INTERNAL ANATOMY OF A FEMALE LIZARD

Funnel

Esophagus

Ovary

Oviduct

Trachea

Kidney

Ureter

Anterior chamber of cloaca

Heart

Liver

Small intestine

Bladder

Rectum

Cloacal opening

Posterior chamber of cloaca

Hind leg

Tail

33

Crocodilians and turtles

CROCODILIANS AND TURTLES BELONG to different orders in the class Reptilia. The order Crocodilia includes crocodiles, alligators, caimans, and gharials. Typically, crocodilians are carnivores (flesh-eaters), and have a long snout, sharp teeth for gripping prey, and hard, square scales. All crocodilians are adapted to living on land and in water: they have four strong legs for moving on land; a powerful tail for swimming; and their eyes and nostrils are high on the head so that they stay above water while the rest of the body is submerged. The order Chelonia includes marine turtles, freshwater turtles (terrapins), and land turtles (tortoises). Characteristically, chelonians have a short, broad body encased in a bony shell with an outer horny covering, into which the head and limbs can be withdrawn; and a horny beak instead of teeth.

GHARIAL
(Gavialis gangeticus)

NILE CROCODILE
(Crocodylus niloticus)

MISSISSIPPI ALLIGATOR
(Alligator mississippiensis)

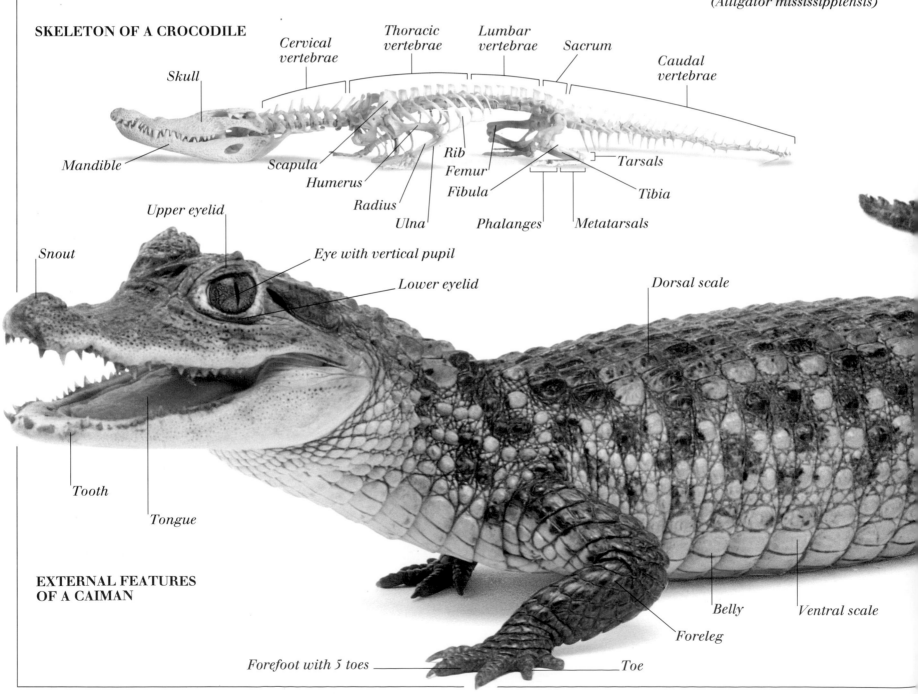

SKELETON OF A CROCODILE

Cervical vertebrae
Thoracic vertebrae
Lumbar vertebrae
Sacrum
Caudal vertebrae
Skull
Mandible
Scapula
Humerus
Radius
Ulna
Rib
Femur
Fibula
Phalanges
Metatarsals
Tarsals
Tibia

Upper eyelid
Eye with vertical pupil
Lower eyelid
Snout
Dorsal scale
Tooth
Tongue

EXTERNAL FEATURES OF A CAIMAN

Belly
Ventral scale
Foreleg
Forefoot with 5 toes
Toe

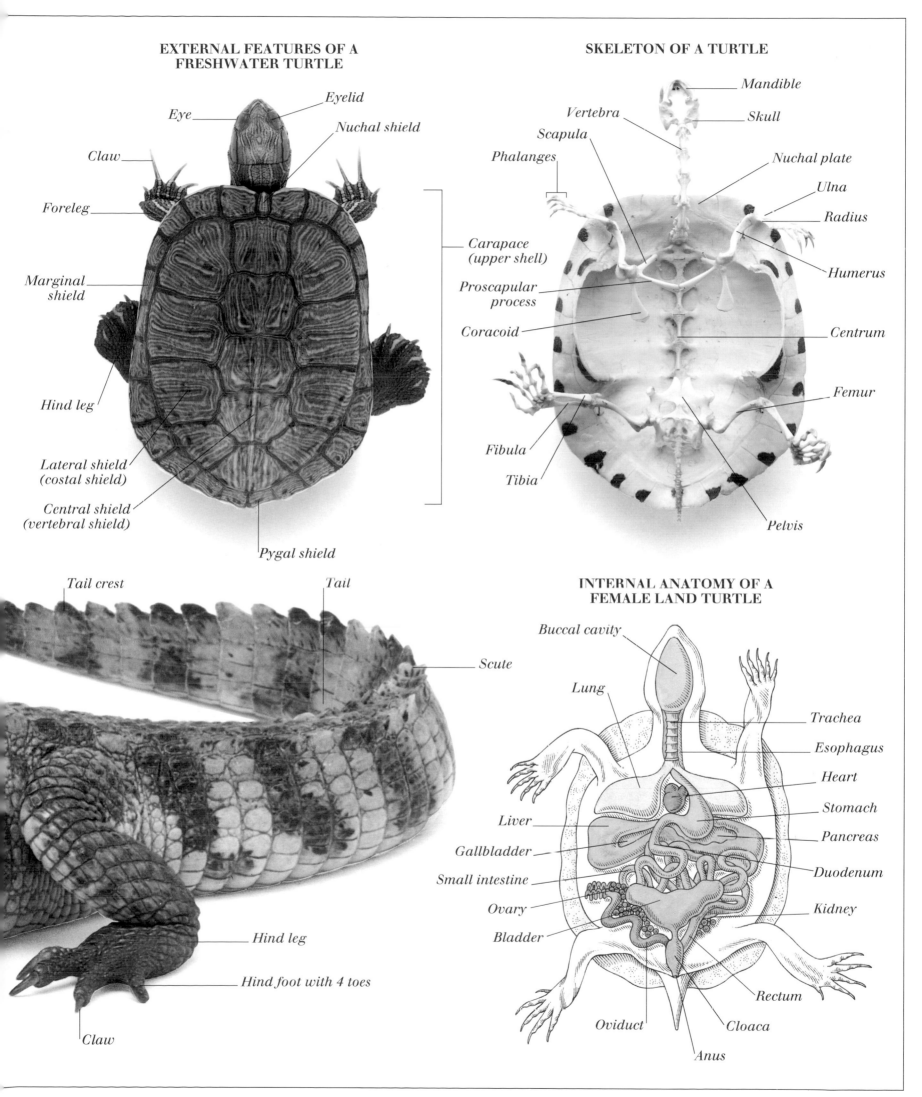

EXTERNAL FEATURES OF A FRESHWATER TURTLE

Eye
Eyelid
Nuchal shield
Claw
Foreleg
Marginal shield
Hind leg
Lateral shield (costal shield)
Central shield (vertebral shield)
Pygal shield
Carapace (upper shell)

SKELETON OF A TURTLE

Mandible
Vertebra
Skull
Scapula
Phalanges
Nuchal plate
Ulna
Radius
Humerus
Proscapular process
Coracoid
Centrum
Femur
Fibula
Tibia
Pelvis

Tail crest
Tail
Scute
Hind leg
Hind foot with 4 toes
Claw

INTERNAL ANATOMY OF A FEMALE LAND TURTLE

Buccal cavity
Lung
Trachea
Esophagus
Heart
Stomach
Pancreas
Liver
Gallbladder
Duodenum
Small intestine
Ovary
Kidney
Bladder
Rectum
Oviduct
Cloaca
Anus

Birds 1

BIRDS MAKE UP THE CLASS AVES. There are more than 9,000 species, almost all of which can fly (the only flightless birds are penguins, ostriches, rheas, cassowaries, and kiwis). The ability to fly is reflected in the typical bird features: forelimbs modified as wings, a streamlined body, and hollow bones to reduce weight. All birds lay hard-shelled eggs, which the parents incubate. Birds' beaks and feet vary according to diet and way of life. Beaks range from general purpose types suitable for a mixed diet (those of thrushes, for example), to types specialized for particular foods (such as the large, curved, sieving beaks of flamingos). Feet range from the webbed "paddles" of ducks, to the talons of birds of prey. Plumage also varies widely, and in many species the male is brightly colored for courtship display whereas the female is drab.

EXTERNAL FEATURES OF A BIRD

Forehead
Eye
Crown
Nostril
Nape
Upper mandible
Beak
Lower mandible
Chin
Throat

EXAMPLES OF BIRDS

MALE TUFTED DUCK
(*Aythya fuligula*)

WHITE STORK
(*Ciconia ciconia*)

MALE OSTRICH
(*Struthio camelus*)

Minor coverts
Lesser wing coverts
Median wing coverts

Greater wing coverts (major coverts)

Secondary flight feathers (secondary remiges)

Primary flight feathers (primary remiges)

Breast

Belly

Flank

Thigh

Claw

Under tail coverts

Tarsus

Toe

Tail feathers (retrices)

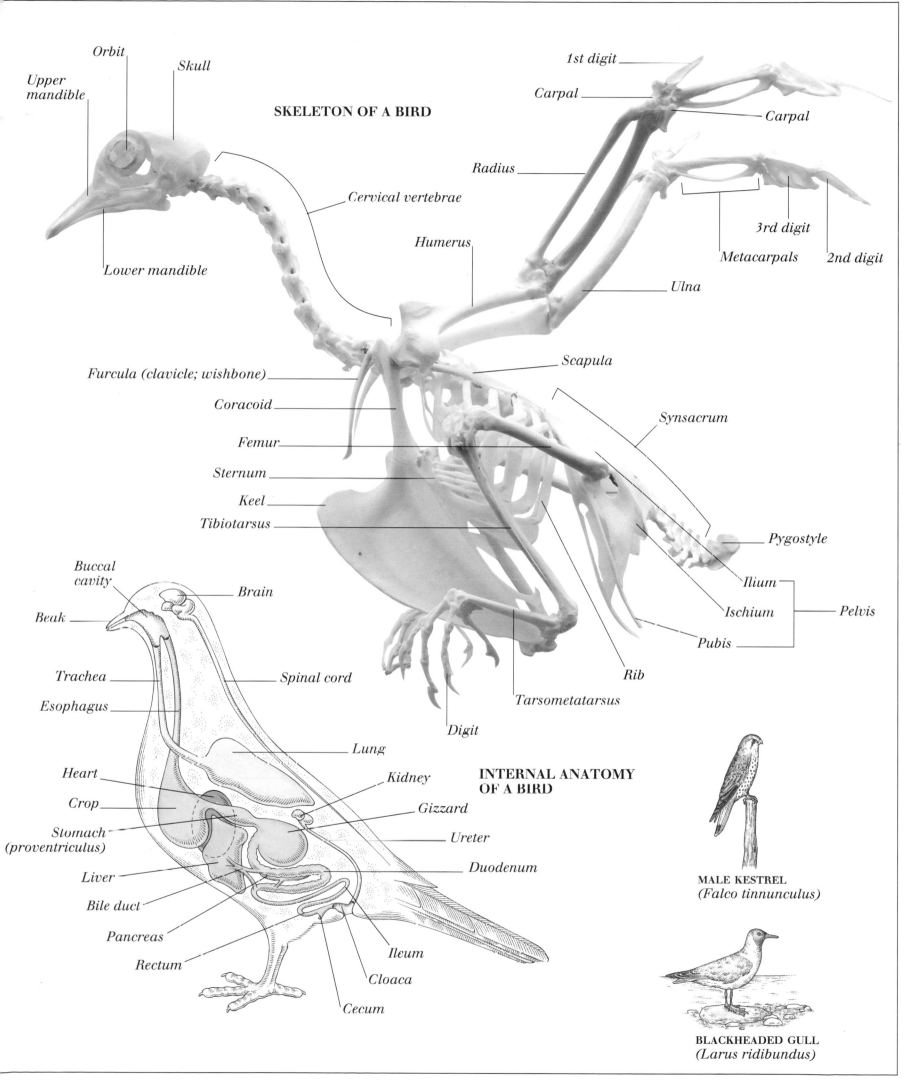

SKELETON OF A BIRD

Upper mandible

Orbit

Skull

Lower mandible

Cervical vertebrae

Humerus

1st digit

Carpal

Carpal

Radius

3rd digit

Metacarpals

2nd digit

Ulna

Furcula (clavicle; wishbone)

Coracoid

Scapula

Femur

Synsacrum

Sternum

Keel

Tibiotarsus

Pygostyle

Ilium

Ischium

Pelvis

Pubis

Rib

Tarsometatarsus

Digit

INTERNAL ANATOMY OF A BIRD

Buccal cavity

Brain

Beak

Trachea

Spinal cord

Esophagus

Lung

Heart

Kidney

Crop

Gizzard

Stomach (proventriculus)

Ureter

Liver

Duodenum

Bile duct

Pancreas

Ileum

Rectum

Cloaca

Cecum

MALE KESTREL
(Falco tinnunculus)

BLACKHEADED GULL
(Larus ridibundus)

Birds 2

EXAMPLES OF BIRDS' FEET

KITTIWAKE
(Rissa tridactyla)
The webbed feet are
adapted for paddling
through water.

LITTLE GREBE
(Tachybaptus ruficollis)
The lobed, flattened feet
are adapted for swimming
underwater.

TAWNY OWL
(Strix aluco)
The clawed feet are adapted
for gripping prey.

EXAMPLES OF BIRDS' BEAKS

KING VULTURE
(Sarcorhamphus papa)
The hooked beak is adapted
for pulling apart flesh.

GREATER FLAMINGO
(Phoenicopterus ruber)
In the living bird, the large,
curved beak contains a
cartilaginous "sieve" for
filtering food particles
from water.

MAVIS, OR MISTLE THRUSH
(Turdus viscivorus)
The all-purpose beak is suitable
for gathering a wide range of
animal and plant foods.

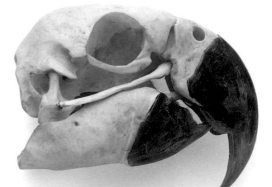

BLUE-AND-YELLOW MACAW
(Ara ararauna)
The broad, powerful, hooked beak
is adapted for crushing seeds and
eating fruit.

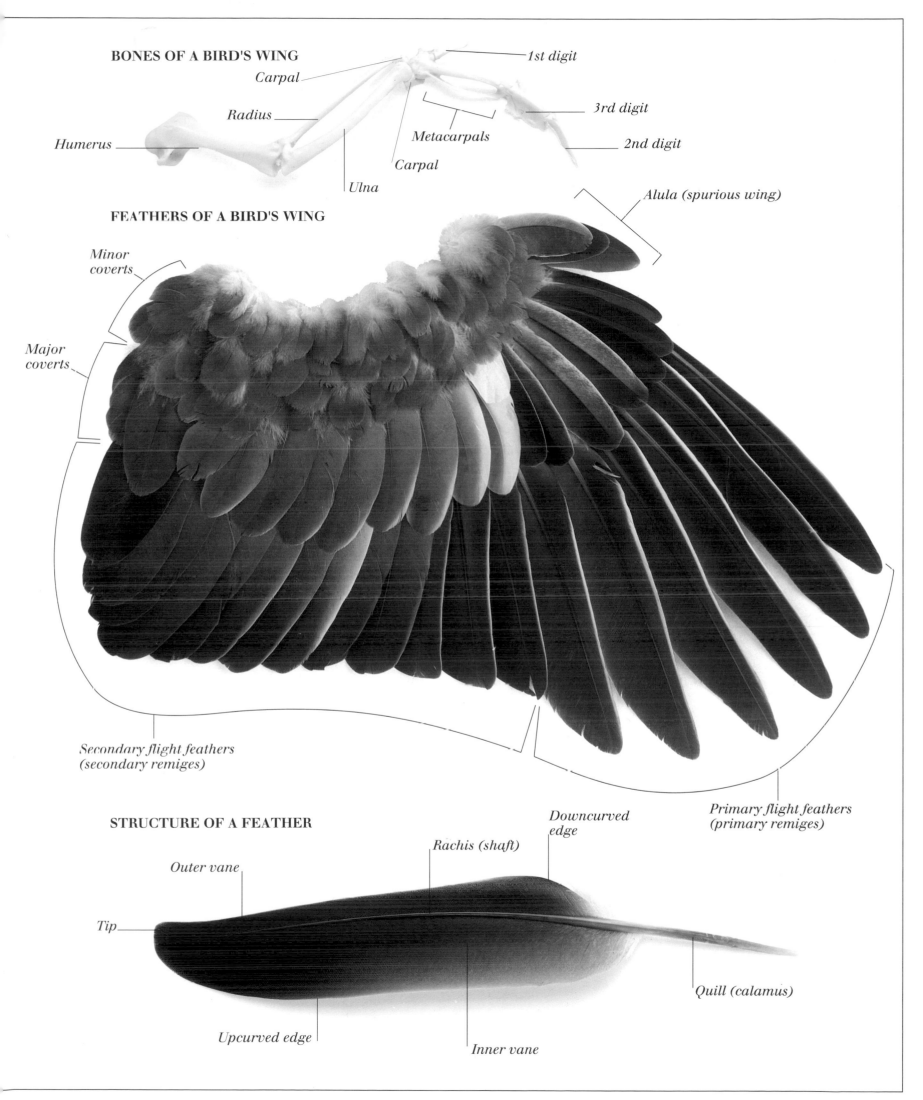

BONES OF A BIRD'S WING

1st digit

Carpal

Radius

3rd digit

Metacarpals

Humerus

2nd digit

Carpal

Ulna

Alula (spurious wing)

FEATHERS OF A BIRD'S WING

Minor
coverts

Major
coverts

Secondary flight feathers
(secondary remiges)

Downcurved
edge

Primary flight feathers
(primary remiges)

STRUCTURE OF A FEATHER

Rachis (shaft)

Outer vane

Tip

Quill (calamus)

Upcurved edge

Inner vane

Eggs

AN EGG IS A SINGLE CELL, produced by the female, with the capacity to develop into a new individual. Development may take place inside the mother's body (as in most mammals) or outside, in which case the egg has a protective covering such as a shell. Egg yolk nourishes the growing young. Eggs developing inside the mother generally have little yolk, because the young are nourished from her body. Eggs developing outside may also have little yolk if they are produced by animals whose young go through a larval stage (such as a caterpillar) that feeds itself while developing into the adult form. The shelled eggs of birds and reptiles contain enough yolk to sustain the young until it hatches into a juvenile version of the adult.

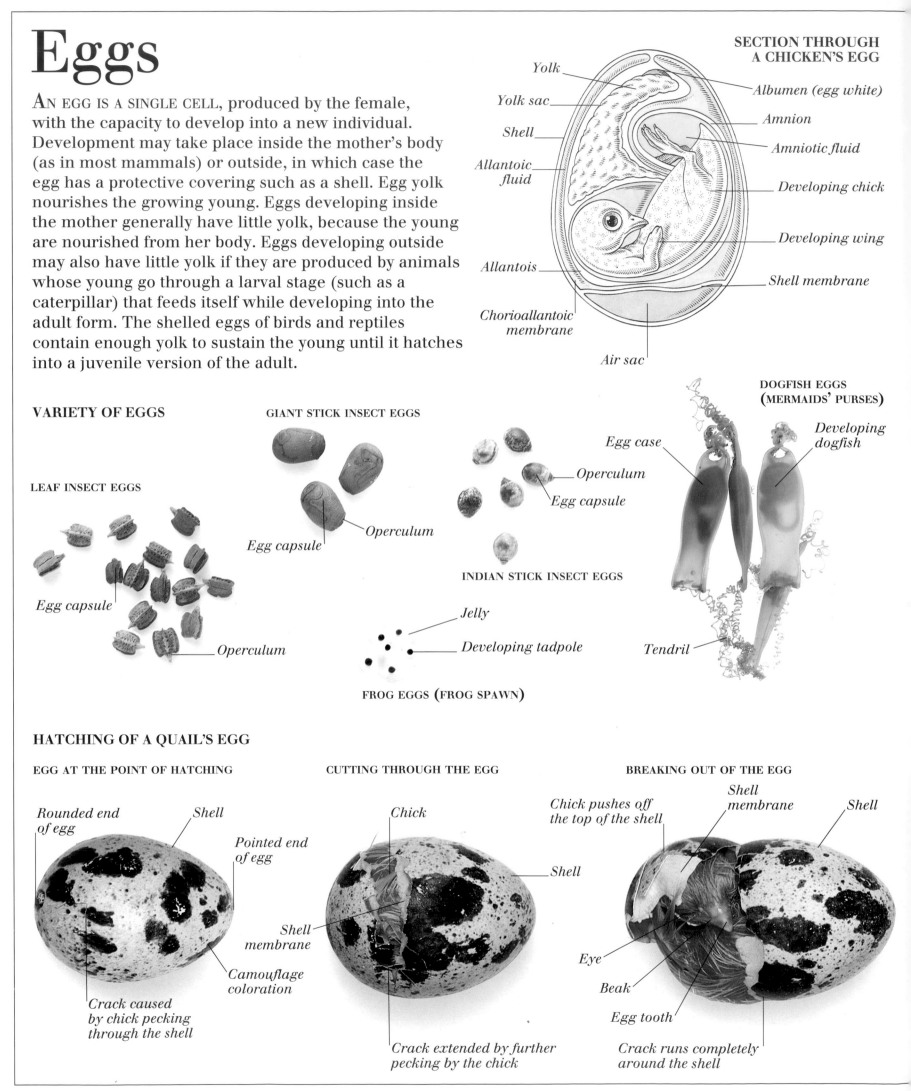

SECTION THROUGH A CHICKEN'S EGG

Yolk

Yolk sac

Shell

Allantoic fluid

Allantois

Chorioallantoic membrane

Air sac

Albumen (egg white)

Amnion

Amniotic fluid

Developing chick

Developing wing

Shell membrane

VARIETY OF EGGS

LEAF INSECT EGGS

Egg capsule

Operculum

GIANT STICK INSECT EGGS

Egg capsule

Operculum

INDIAN STICK INSECT EGGS

Operculum

Egg capsule

FROG EGGS (FROG SPAWN)

Jelly

Developing tadpole

DOGFISH EGGS (MERMAIDS' PURSES)

Developing dogfish

Egg case

Tendril

HATCHING OF A QUAIL'S EGG

EGG AT THE POINT OF HATCHING

Rounded end of egg

Shell

Pointed end of egg

Camouflage coloration

Crack caused by chick pecking through the shell

CUTTING THROUGH THE EGG

Chick

Shell

Shell membrane

Crack extended by further pecking by the chick

BREAKING OUT OF THE EGG

Chick pushes off the top of the shell

Shell membrane

Shell

Eye

Beak

Egg tooth

Crack runs completely around the shell

EXAMPLES OF BIRDS' EGGS

BEE HUMMINGBIRD
(Calypte helenae)

GREATER BLACKBACKED GULL
(Larus marinus)

BALTIMORE ORIOLE
(Icterus galbula)

WILLOW GROUSE
(Lagopus lagopus)

COMMON TERN
(Sterna hirundo)

CARRION CROW
(Corvus corone)

CHAFFINCH
(Fringilla coelebs)

OSTRICH
(Struthio camelus)

EMERGING FROM THE EGG

Eye

Beak

Egg tooth

Chick heaves itself out of the egg

Tympanum (eardrum)

Shell

Wet down

Remains of egg membranes (amnion and allantois)

THE NEWLY HATCHED CHICK

Eye

Beak

Egg tooth

Nostril

Tympanum (eardrum)

Chick is dry about an hour after hatching

Dry down

Toe

Claw

Leg

Eggshell

41

Carnivores

THE MAMMALIAN ORDER CARNIVORA includes cats, dogs, bears, raccoons, pandas, weasels, badgers, skunks, otters, civets, mongooses, and hyenas. The order's name is derived from the fact that most of its members are carnivores (flesh-eaters). Typical carnivore features therefore reflect a hunting life-style: speed and agility; sharp claws and well-developed canine teeth for holding and killing prey; carnassial teeth (cheek teeth) for cutting flesh; and forward-facing eyes for good distance judgment. However, some members of the order—bears, badgers, and foxes, for example—have a more mixed diet, and a few are entirely herbivorous (plant-eating), notably pandas. Such animals have no carnassial teeth and tend to be slower-moving than pure flesh-eaters.

EXTERNAL FEATURES OF A MALE LION

Nose

Eye

Mane

Nostril

Vibrissa (whisker)

Tongue

Canine tooth

Incisor tooth

Chest

Elbow

Lower arm

Toe

SKULL OF A LION

Zygomatic arch

Coronoid process

Sagittal crest

Orbit

Nasal bone

Maxilla

Upper premolars

Upper canine

Lower canine

Mandible

Lower premolars

Occipital condyle

Tympanic bulla

Condyle

Angular process

Upper carnassial tooth (4th upper premolar)

SKULL OF A BEAR

Sagittal crest

Occipital condyle

Zygomatic arch

Orbit

Upper molars

Nasal bone

Upper premolars

Maxilla

Upper canine

Upper incisor

Lower incisor

Lower canine

Mandible

Lower premolars

Tympanic bulla

Angular process

Condyle

Lower molars

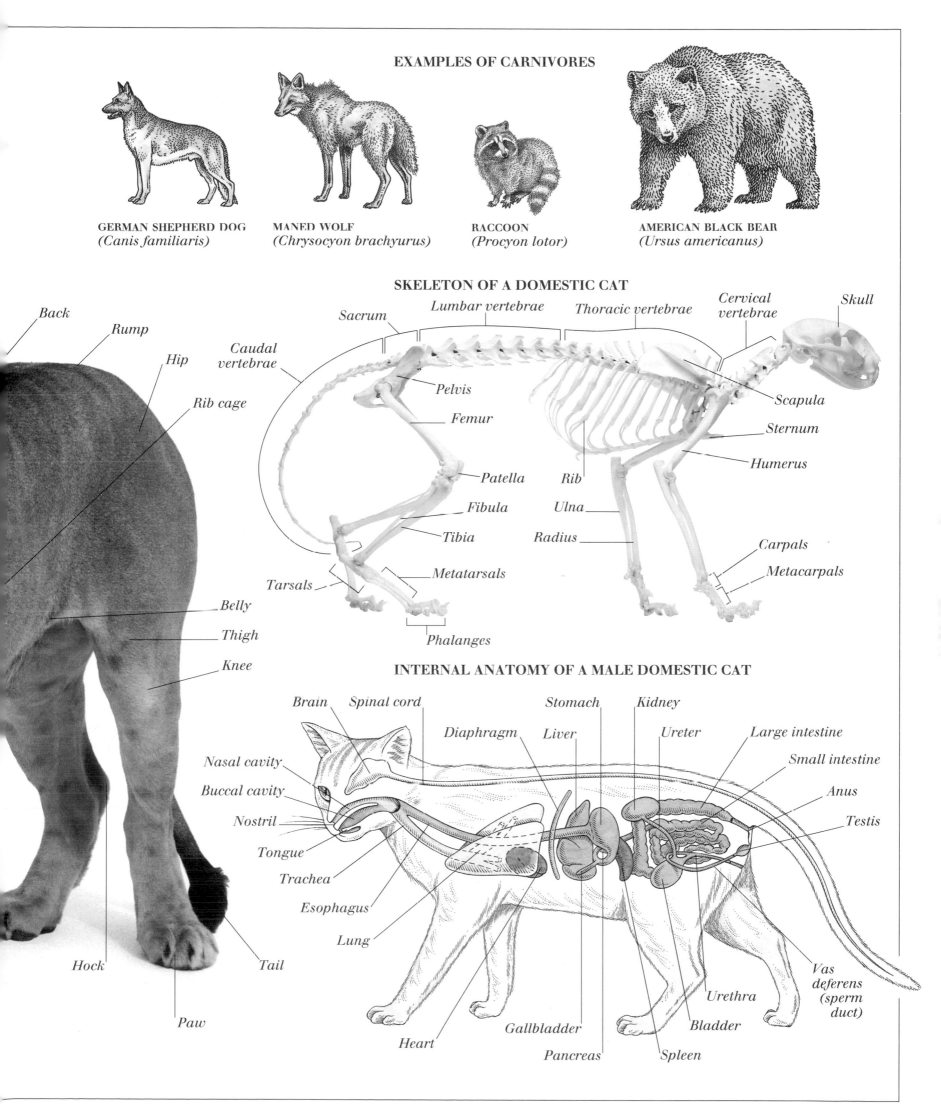

EXAMPLES OF CARNIVORES

GERMAN SHEPHERD DOG
(Canis familiaris)

MANED WOLF
(Chrysocyon brachyurus)

RACCOON
(Procyon lotor)

AMERICAN BLACK BEAR
(Ursus americanus)

SKELETON OF A DOMESTIC CAT

Back

Rump

Hip

Rib cage

Sacrum

Lumbar vertebrae

Thoracic vertebrae

Cervical vertebrae

Skull

Caudal vertebrae

Pelvis

Femur

Scapula

Sternum

Humerus

Patella

Rib

Fibula

Ulna

Tibia

Radius

Carpals

Metatarsals

Metacarpals

Tarsals

Belly

Thigh

Knee

Phalanges

Hock

Tail

Paw

INTERNAL ANATOMY OF A MALE DOMESTIC CAT

Brain

Spinal cord

Stomach

Kidney

Diaphragm

Liver

Ureter

Large intestine

Nasal cavity

Small intestine

Buccal cavity

Anus

Nostril

Testis

Tongue

Trachea

Esophagus

Lung

Vas deferens (sperm duct)

Heart

Gallbladder

Pancreas

Urethra

Spleen

Bladder

Rabbits and rodents

ALTHOUGH RABBITS AND RODENTS belong to different orders of mammals, they have some features in common. These features include chisel-shaped incisor teeth that grow continually, and eating their feces to extract more nutrients from their plant diet. Rabbits and hares belong to the order Lagomorpha. Characteristically, they have four incisors in the upper jaw and two in the lower jaw; powerful hind legs for jumping; forelimbs adapted for burrowing; long ears; and a small tail. Rodents make up the order Rodentia. This is the largest order of mammals, with more than 1,700 species, including squirrels, beavers, chipmunks, gophers, rats, mice, lemmings, gerbils, porcupines, cavies, and the capybara. Typical rodent features include two incisors in each jaw; short forelimbs for manipulating food; and cheek pouches for storing food.

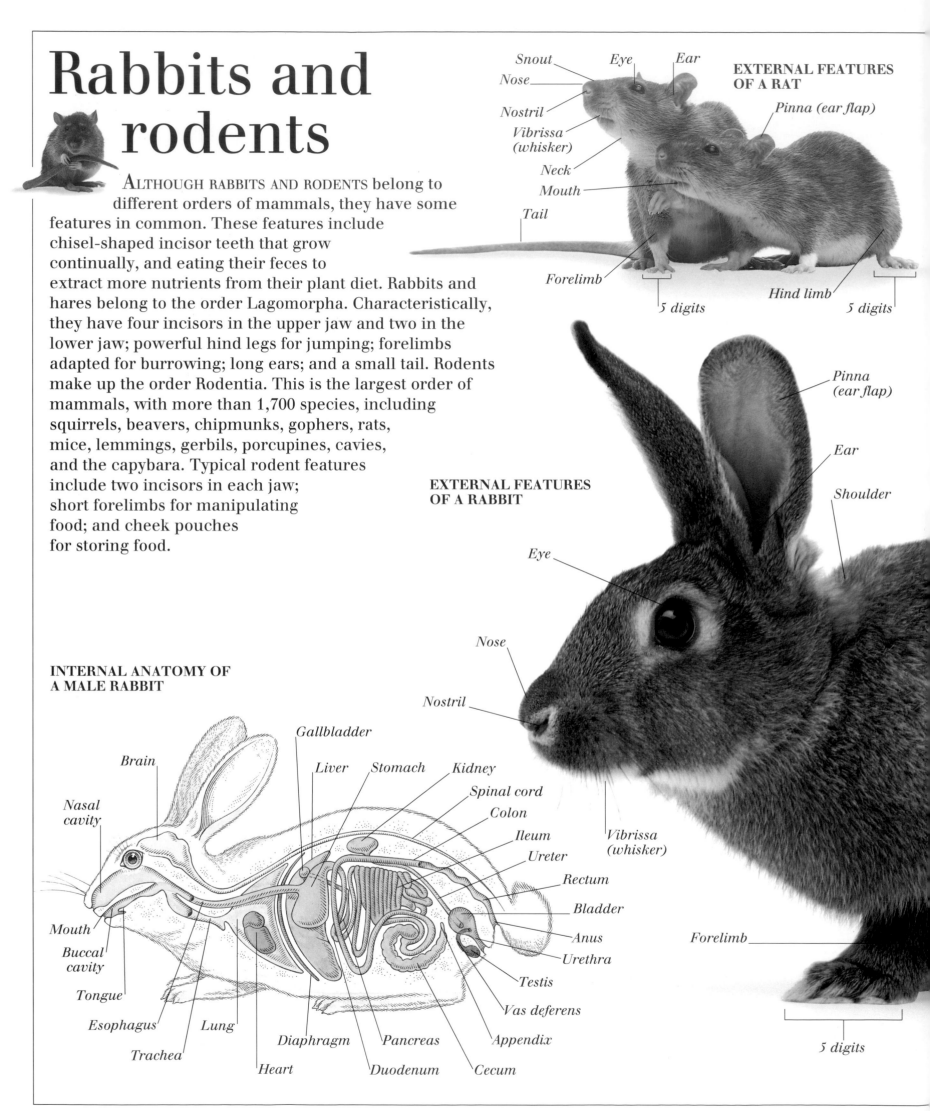

EXTERNAL FEATURES OF A RAT

Snout
Eye
Ear
Pinna (ear flap)
Nose
Nostril
Vibrissa (whisker)
Neck
Mouth
Tail
Forelimb
5 digits
Hind limb
5 digits

EXTERNAL FEATURES OF A RABBIT

Pinna (ear flap)
Ear
Shoulder
Eye
Nose
Nostril
Vibrissa (whisker)
Forelimb
5 digits

INTERNAL ANATOMY OF A MALE RABBIT

Brain
Gallbladder
Liver
Stomach
Kidney
Spinal cord
Colon
Ileum
Ureter
Rectum
Bladder
Anus
Urethra
Testis
Vas deferens
Appendix
Cecum
Duodenum
Pancreas
Diaphragm
Heart
Trachea
Esophagus
Lung
Tongue
Buccal cavity
Mouth
Nasal cavity

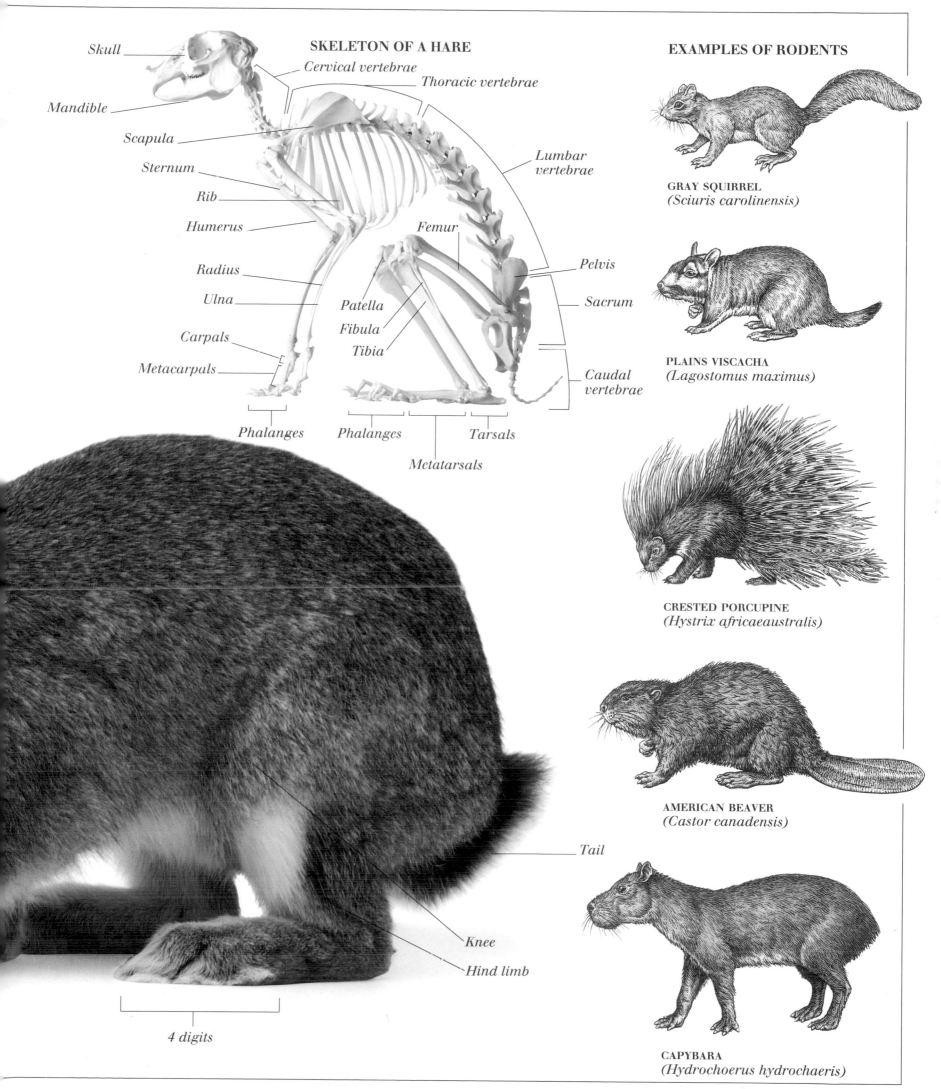

SKELETON OF A HARE

Skull

Mandible

Cervical vertebrae

Thoracic vertebrae

Scapula

Sternum

Rib

Humerus

Lumbar vertebrae

Radius

Femur

Ulna

Pelvis

Patella

Carpals

Fibula

Sacrum

Metacarpals

Tibia

Caudal vertebrae

Phalanges

Phalanges

Tarsals

Metatarsals

Tail

Knee

Hind limb

4 digits

EXAMPLES OF RODENTS

GRAY SQUIRREL
(Sciuris carolinensis)

PLAINS VISCACHA
(Lagostomus maximus)

CRESTED PORCUPINE
(Hystrix africaeaustralis)

AMERICAN BEAVER
(Castor canadensis)

CAPYBARA
(Hydrochoerus hydrochaeris)

Ungulates

UNGULATES IS A GENERAL TERM FOR a large, varied group of mammals that includes horses, cattle, and their relatives. The ungulates are divided into two orders on the basis of the number of toes. Members of the order Perissodactyla (odd-toed ungulates) have one or three toes. Perissodactyls include horses, asses, and zebras (all of which are one-toed), and rhinoceroses and tapirs (which are three-toed). Members of the order Artiodactyla (even-toed ungulates) have two or four toes. Most artiodactyls have two toes, which are typically encased in hooves to give the so-called cloven hoof. Two-toed, cloven-hoofed artiodactyls include cows and other cattle, sheep, goats, antelopes, deer, and giraffes. The other main two-toed artiodactyls are camels and llamas. Most two-toed artiodactyls are ruminants; that is, they have a four-chambered stomach and chew the cud. The principal four-toed artiodactyls are hogs and hippopotamuses.

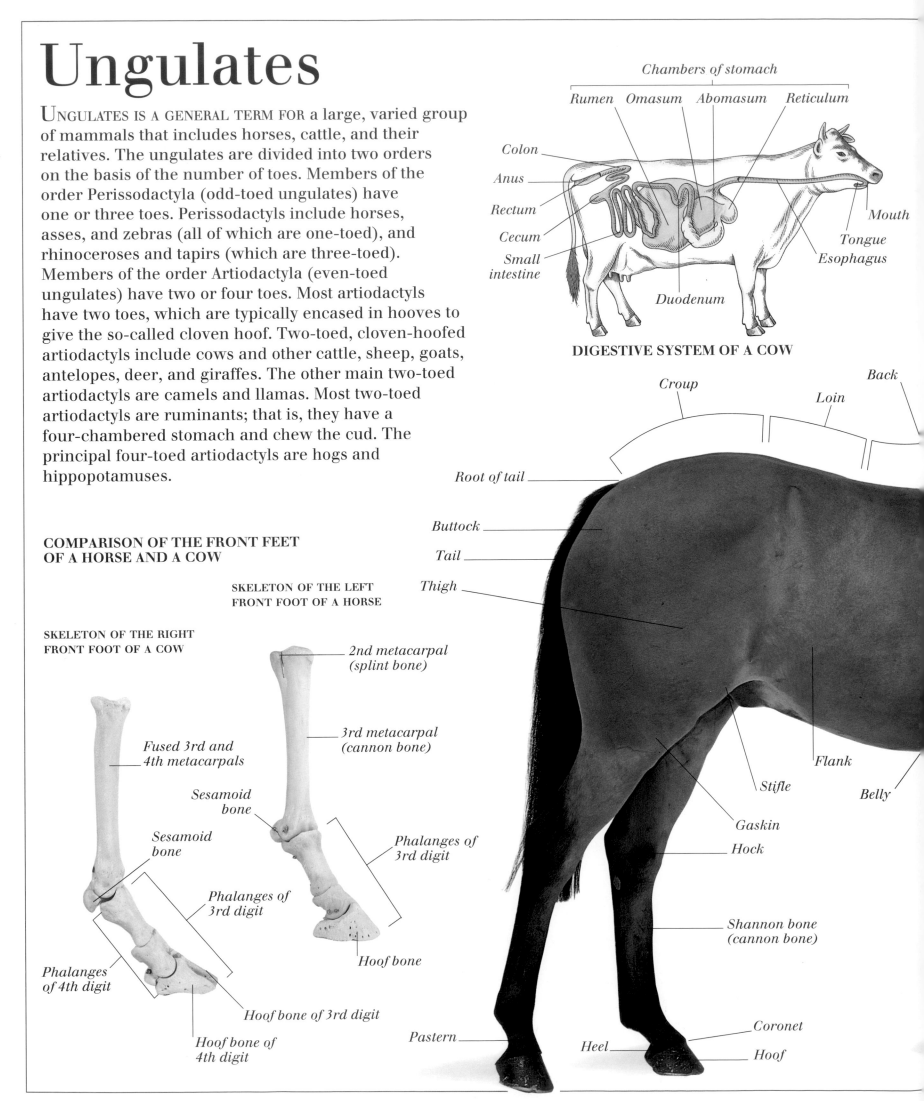

Chambers of stomach

Rumen Omasum Abomasum Reticulum

Colon

Anus

Rectum

Cecum

Small intestine

Duodenum

Mouth

Tongue

Esophagus

DIGESTIVE SYSTEM OF A COW

COMPARISON OF THE FRONT FEET OF A HORSE AND A COW

SKELETON OF THE LEFT FRONT FOOT OF A HORSE

SKELETON OF THE RIGHT FRONT FOOT OF A COW

2nd metacarpal (splint bone)

3rd metacarpal (cannon bone)

Fused 3rd and 4th metacarpals

Sesamoid bone

Sesamoid bone

Phalanges of 3rd digit

Phalanges of 3rd digit

Phalanges of 4th digit

Hoof bone

Hoof bone of 3rd digit

Hoof bone of 4th digit

Pastern

Croup

Loin

Back

Root of tail

Buttock

Tail

Thigh

Flank

Belly

Stifle

Gaskin

Hock

Shannon bone (cannon bone)

Coronet

Heel

Hoof

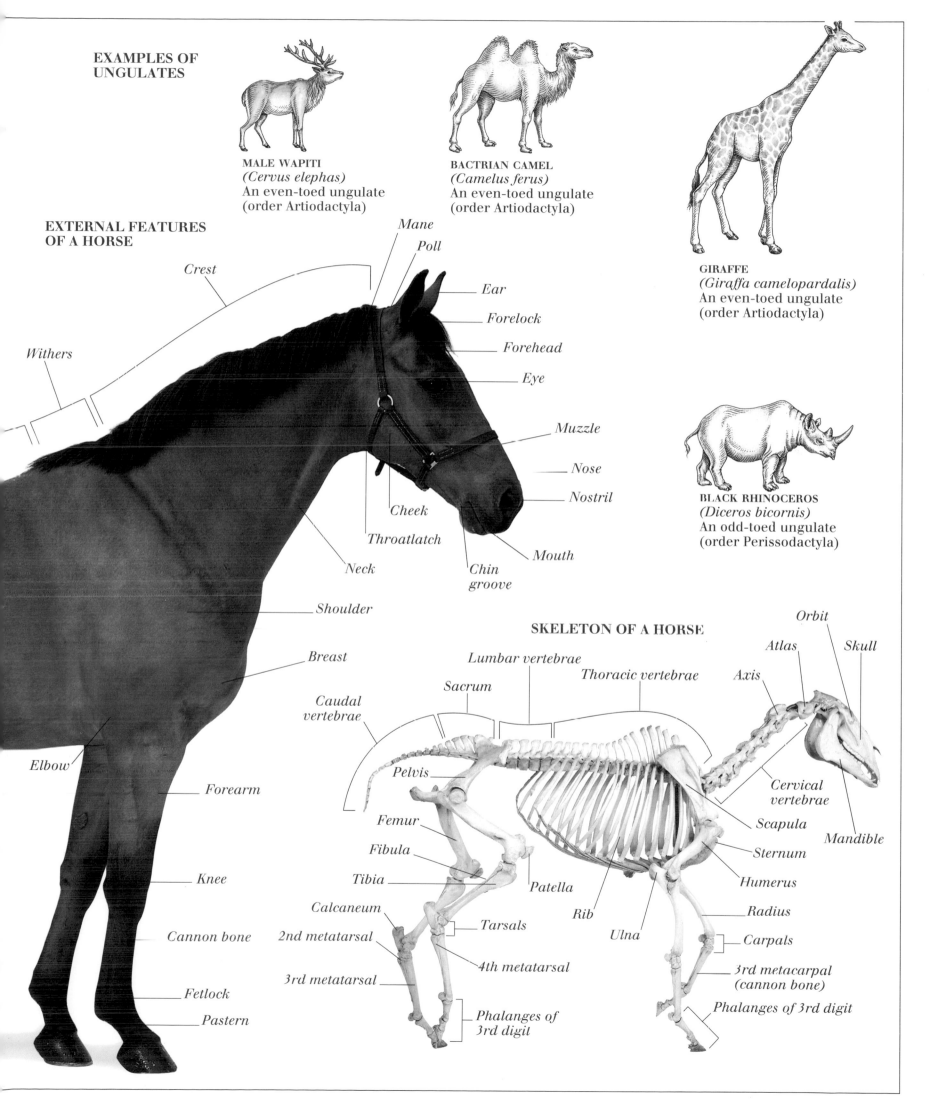

EXAMPLES OF UNGULATES

MALE WAPITI
(Cervus elephas)
An even-toed ungulate
(order Artiodactyla)

BACTRIAN CAMEL
(Camelus ferus)
An even-toed ungulate
(order Artiodactyla)

GIRAFFE
(Giraffa camelopardalis)
An even-toed ungulate
(order Artiodactyla)

BLACK RHINOCEROS
(Diceros bicornis)
An odd-toed ungulate
(order Perissodactyla)

EXTERNAL FEATURES OF A HORSE

Crest

Withers

Mane

Poll

Ear

Forelock

Forehead

Eye

Muzzle

Nose

Nostril

Cheek

Throatlatch

Mouth

Chin groove

Neck

Shoulder

Breast

Elbow

Forearm

Knee

Cannon bone

Fetlock

Pastern

SKELETON OF A HORSE

Lumbar vertebrae

Thoracic vertebrae

Orbit

Atlas

Skull

Axis

Sacrum

Caudal vertebrae

Pelvis

Femur

Fibula

Tibia

Calcaneum

2nd metatarsal

Tarsals

4th metatarsal

3rd metatarsal

Phalanges of 3rd digit

Patella

Rib

Cervical vertebrae

Scapula

Sternum

Humerus

Ulna

Radius

Carpals

3rd metacarpal (cannon bone)

Phalanges of 3rd digit

Mandible

Elephants

THE TWO SPECIES of elephants—African and Asian—are the only members of the mammalian order Proboscidea. The bigger African elephant is the largest land animal: a fully grown male may be up to 13 ft (4m) tall and weigh as much as 7.7 tons (7 tonnes). A fully grown male Asian elephant may be 11 ft (3.3 m) tall and weigh 6 tons (5.4 tonnes). The trunk—an extension of the nose and upper lip—is the elephant's other most obvious feature. It is used for manipulating and lifting, feeding, drinking and spraying water, smelling, touching, and producing trumpeting sounds. Other characteristic features include a pair of tusks, used for defense and for crushing vegetation; thick, pillar-like legs and broad feet to support the massive body; and large ear flaps that act as radiators to keep the elephant cool.

DIFFERENCES BETWEEN AFRICAN AND ASIAN ELEPHANTS

Flat forehead
Concave back
Very large ears
2 "lips" at the end of the trunk
4 toenails
3 toenails

AFRICAN ELEPHANT
(Loxodonta africana)

Twin-domed forehead
Arched back
Smaller ears
1 "lip" at the end of the trunk
5 toenails
4 toenails

ASIAN ELEPHANT
(Elephas maximus)

INTERNAL ANATOMY OF A FEMALE ELEPHANT

Duodenum
Spinal cord
Heart
Stomach
Kidney
Ureter
Uterus
Rump
Brain
Rectum
Nasal cavity
Bladder
Buccal cavity
Anal flap
Anus
Mouth
Vagina
Tongue
Epiglottis
Tusk
Esophagus
Trachea
Hind leg
Lung
Small intestine
Nasal passage
Diaphragm
Spleen
Vulva
Toenail
Nostril

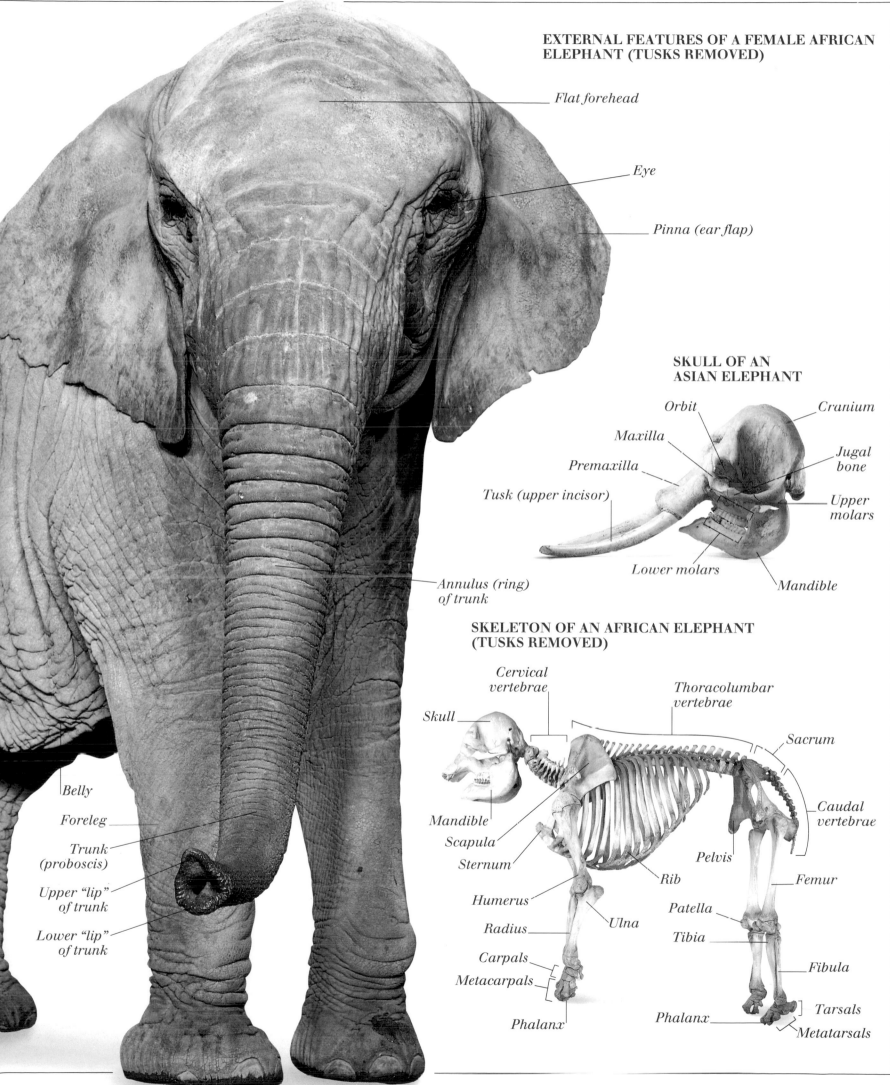

EXTERNAL FEATURES OF A FEMALE AFRICAN ELEPHANT (TUSKS REMOVED)

Flat forehead

Eye

Pinna (ear flap)

Annulus (ring) of trunk

Belly

Foreleg

Trunk (proboscis)

Upper "lip" of trunk

Lower "lip" of trunk

SKULL OF AN ASIAN ELEPHANT

Orbit

Cranium

Maxilla

Jugal bone

Premaxilla

Tusk (upper incisor)

Upper molars

Lower molars

Mandible

SKELETON OF AN AFRICAN ELEPHANT (TUSKS REMOVED)

Cervical vertebrae

Thoracolumbar vertebrae

Skull

Sacrum

Mandible

Scapula

Caudal vertebrae

Sternum

Pelvis

Rib

Femur

Humerus

Patella

Ulna

Tibia

Radius

Fibula

Carpals

Metacarpals

Tarsals

Phalanx

Phalanx

Metatarsals

49

Primates

THE MAMMALIAN ORDER PRIMATES consists of monkeys, apes, and their relatives (including humans). There are two suborders of primates: Prosimii, the primitive primates, which include lemurs, tarsiers, and lorises; and Anthropoidea, the advanced primates, which include monkeys, apes, and humans. The anthropoids are divided into New World monkeys, Old World monkeys, and hominids. New World monkeys typically have widespread nostrils that open to the side; and long tails, which are prehensile (grasping) in some species. This group of monkeys lives in South America, and includes marmosets, tamarins, and howler monkeys. Old World monkeys typically have close-set nostrils that open forward or downward and nonprehensile tails. This group of monkeys lives in Africa and Asia, and includes langurs, mandrills, macaques, and baboons. Hominids typically have large brains and no tail. This group includes the apes—chimpanzees, gibbons, gorillas, and orangutans—and humans.

INTERNAL ANATOMY OF A FEMALE CHIMPANZEE

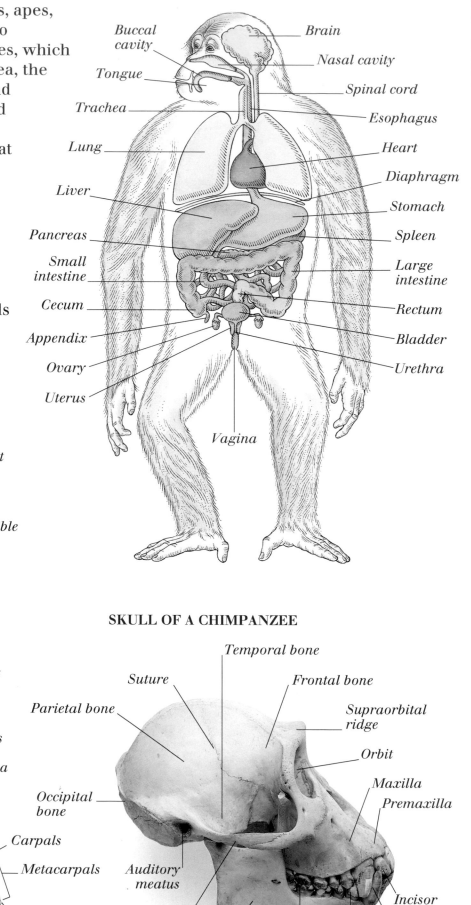

Buccal cavity
Brain
Tongue
Nasal cavity
Trachea
Spinal cord
Lung
Esophagus
Liver
Heart
Pancreas
Diaphragm
Small intestine
Stomach
Cecum
Spleen
Appendix
Large intestine
Ovary
Rectum
Uterus
Bladder
Vagina
Urethra

SKELETON OF A RHESUS MONKEY

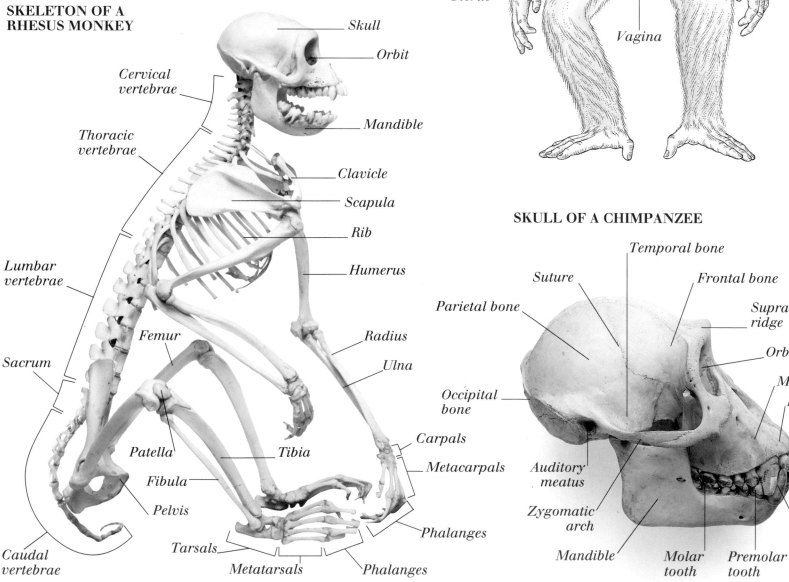

Skull
Orbit
Cervical vertebrae
Mandible
Thoracic vertebrae
Clavicle
Scapula
Rib
Humerus
Lumbar vertebrae
Sacrum
Radius
Ulna
Femur
Patella
Tibia
Carpals
Metacarpals
Fibula
Pelvis
Phalanges
Caudal vertebrae
Tarsals
Metatarsals
Phalanges

SKULL OF A CHIMPANZEE

Temporal bone
Suture
Frontal bone
Parietal bone
Supraorbital ridge
Orbit
Occipital bone
Maxilla
Premaxilla
Auditory meatus
Zygomatic arch
Incisor tooth
Mandible
Molar tooth
Premolar tooth
Canine tooth

EXAMPLES OF PRIMATES

RING-TAILED LEMUR
(Lemur catta)
A prosimian

MALE RED HOWLER MONKEY
(Alouatta seniculus)
A New World monkey

MALE MANDRILL
(Mandrillus sphinx)
An Old World monkey

CHIMPANZEE
(Pan troglodytes)
An ape

EXTERNAL FEATURES OF A YOUNG GORILLA

GOLDEN LION TAMARIN
(Leontopithecus rosalia)
A New World monkey

Pinna (ear flap)

Brow ridge

Shoulder

Eye

Nostril

Mouth

Upper arm

Thigh

Forearm

Chest

Knee

Elbow

Lower leg

Hand

Foot

Toe

Finger

Toenail

51

Dolphins, whales, and seals

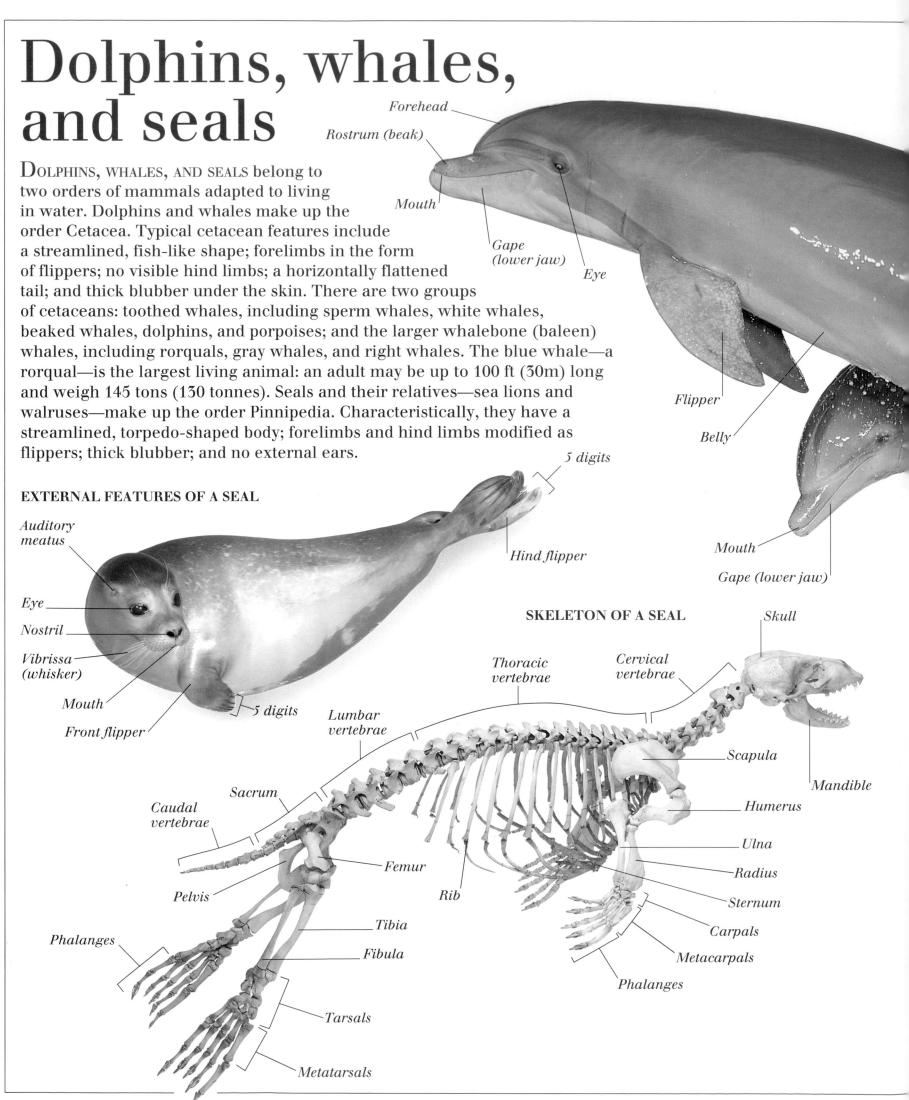

DOLPHINS, WHALES, AND SEALS belong to two orders of mammals adapted to living in water. Dolphins and whales make up the order Cetacea. Typical cetacean features include a streamlined, fish-like shape; forelimbs in the form of flippers; no visible hind limbs; a horizontally flattened tail; and thick blubber under the skin. There are two groups of cetaceans: toothed whales, including sperm whales, white whales, beaked whales, dolphins, and porpoises; and the larger whalebone (baleen) whales, including rorquals, gray whales, and right whales. The blue whale—a rorqual—is the largest living animal: an adult may be up to 100 ft (30m) long and weigh 145 tons (130 tonnes). Seals and their relatives—sea lions and walruses—make up the order Pinnipedia. Characteristically, they have a streamlined, torpedo-shaped body; forelimbs and hind limbs modified as flippers; thick blubber; and no external ears.

Forehead

Rostrum (beak)

Mouth

Gape (lower jaw)

Eye

Flipper

Belly

Mouth

Gape (lower jaw)

5 digits

Hind flipper

EXTERNAL FEATURES OF A SEAL

Auditory meatus

Eye

Nostril

Vibrissa (whisker)

Mouth

Front flipper

5 digits

SKELETON OF A SEAL

Skull

Cervical vertebrae

Thoracic vertebrae

Lumbar vertebrae

Scapula

Mandible

Humerus

Ulna

Radius

Sternum

Carpals

Metacarpals

Phalanges

Sacrum

Caudal vertebrae

Pelvis

Femur

Rib

Tibia

Fibula

Phalanges

Tarsals

Metatarsals

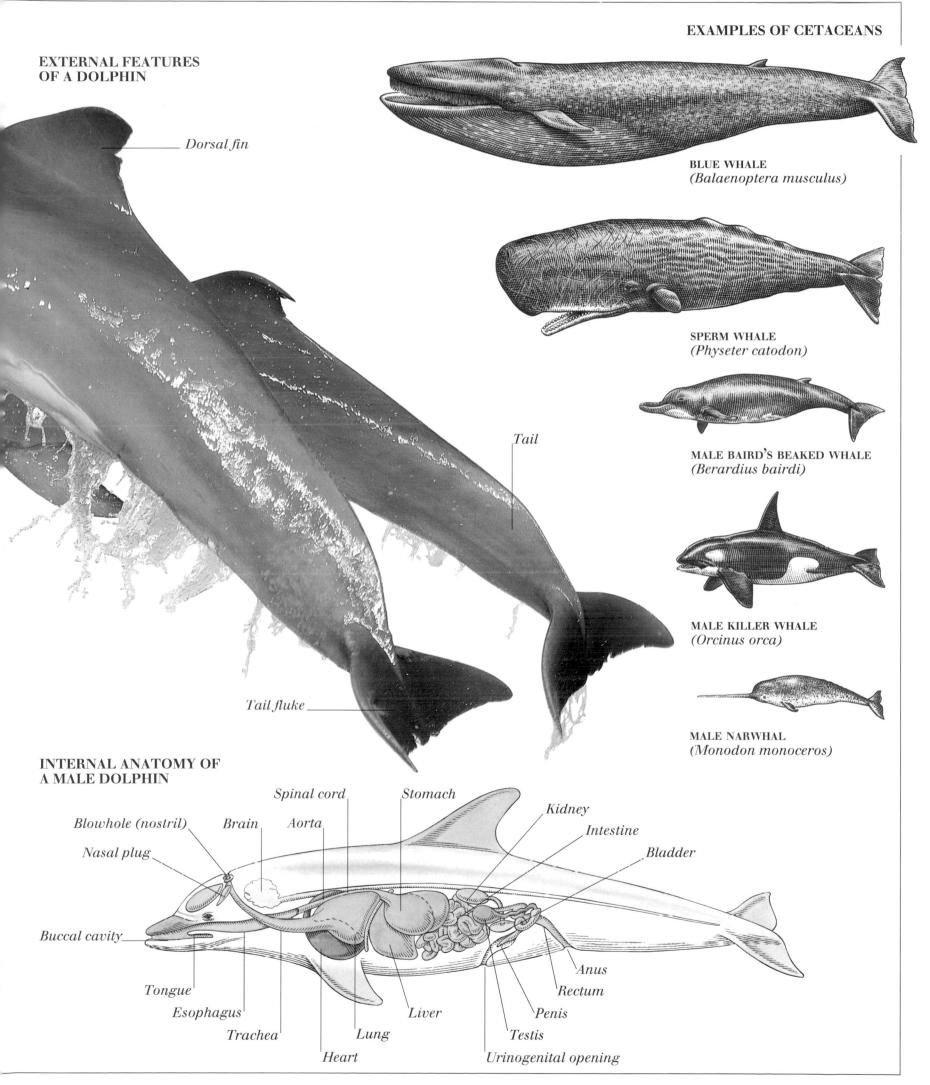

**EXTERNAL FEATURES
OF A DOLPHIN**

Dorsal fin

Tail

Tail fluke

BLUE WHALE
(Balaenoptera musculus)

SPERM WHALE
(Physeter catodon)

MALE BAIRD'S BEAKED WHALE
(Berardius bairdi)

MALE KILLER WHALE
(Orcinus orca)

MALE NARWHAL
(Monodon monoceros)

**INTERNAL ANATOMY OF
A MALE DOLPHIN**

Spinal cord

Stomach

Kidney

Blowhole (nostril)

Brain

Aorta

Intestine

Nasal plug

Bladder

Buccal cavity

Anus

Rectum

Tongue

Penis

Esophagus

Testis

Trachea

Liver

Urinogenital opening

Heart

Lung

Marsupials and Monotremes

MARSUPIALS AND MONOTREMES are two orders of mammals that differ from other mammalian groups in the ways that their young develop. The order Marsupalia, the pouched mammals, is made up of kangaroos and their relatives. Typically, marsupials give birth to their young at a very early stage of development. The young then crawls to the mother's pouch (which is on the outside of her abdomen), where it attaches itself to a nipple and remains until fully developed. Most marsupials live in Australia, although the opossums—which are classified as marsupials despite not having a pouch—live in the Americas. The order Monotremata is made up of the platypus and its relatives (the echidnas, or spiny anteaters). The monotremes are primitive mammals that lay eggs, which the mother incubates. The monotremes are found only in Australia and New Guinea.

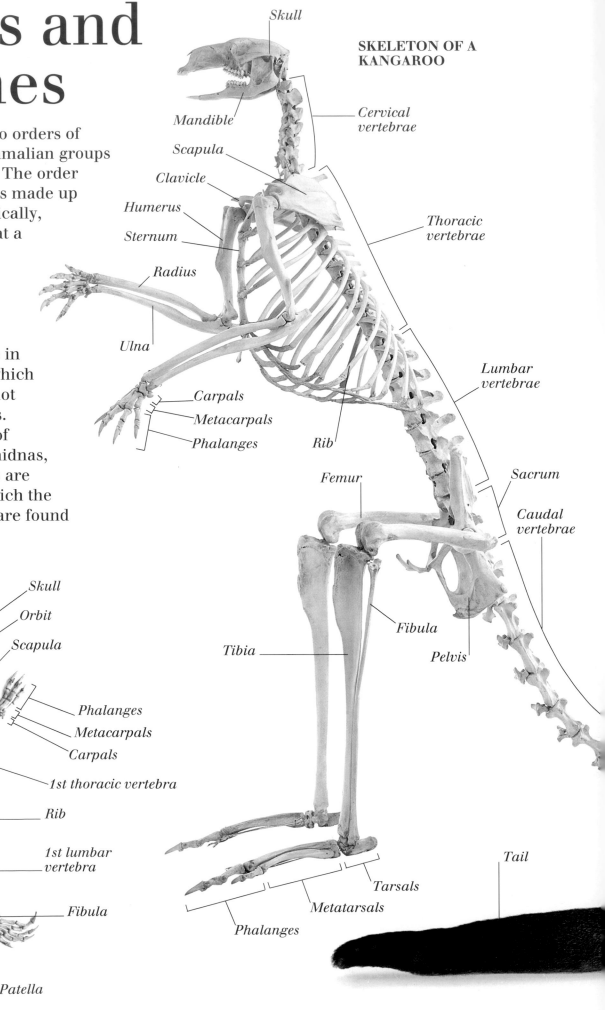

SKELETON OF A KANGAROO

Skull

Mandible

Cervical vertebrae

Scapula

Clavicle

Humerus

Sternum

Thoracic vertebrae

Radius

Ulna

Lumbar vertebrae

Carpals

Metacarpals

Phalanges

Rib

Femur

Sacrum

Caudal vertebrae

Tibia

Fibula

Pelvis

Tarsals

Metatarsals

Phalanges

Tail

SKELETON OF A PLATYPUS

Skull

Orbit

1st cervical vertebra

Scapula

Ulna

Radius

Phalanges

Metacarpals

Carpals

Humerus

1st thoracic vertebra

Rib

1st lumbar vertebra

Femur

Fibula

Tarsals

Metatarsals

Phalanges

Tibia

Patella

Pelvis

1st caudal vertebra

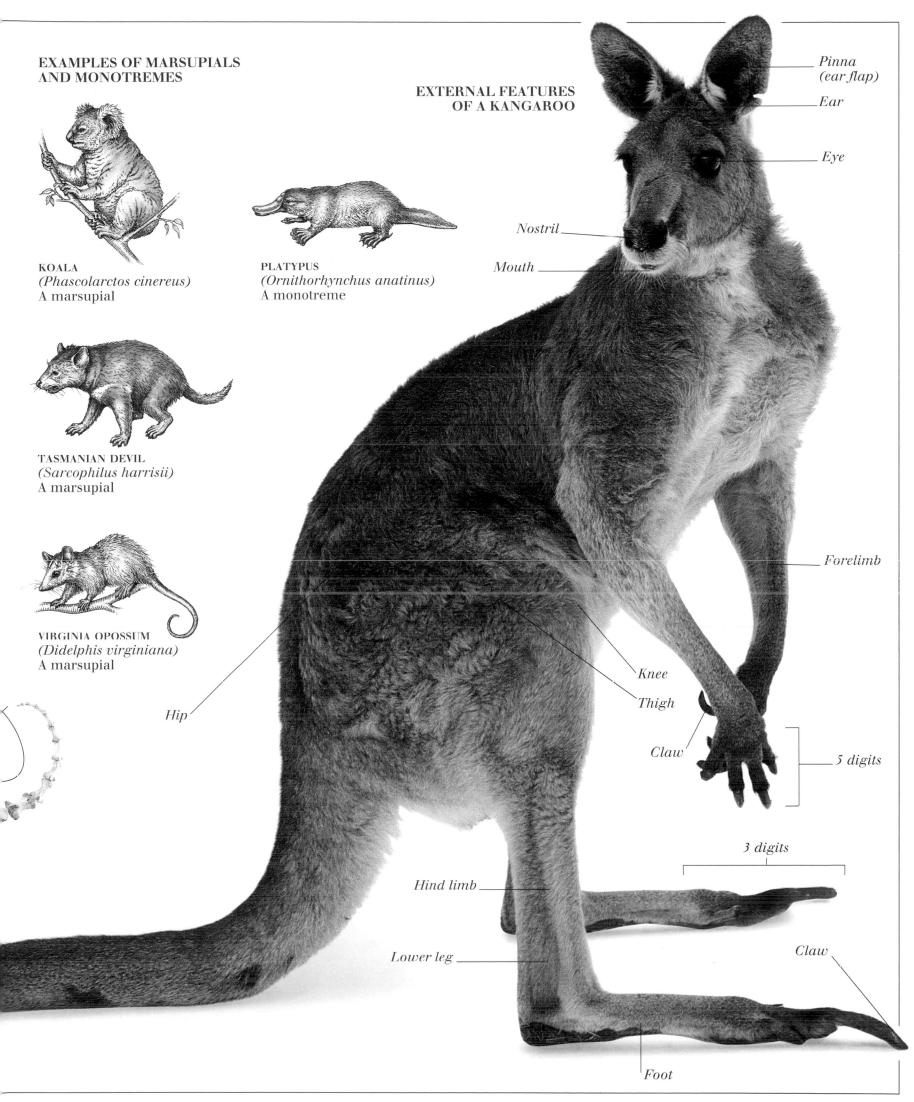

EXAMPLES OF MARSUPIALS AND MONOTREMES

KOALA
(Phascolarctos cinereus)
A marsupial

PLATYPUS
(Ornithorhynchus anatinus)
A monotreme

TASMANIAN DEVIL
(Sarcophilus harrisii)
A marsupial

VIRGINIA OPOSSUM
(Didelphis virginiana)
A marsupial

EXTERNAL FEATURES OF A KANGAROO

Pinna (ear flap)

Ear

Eye

Nostril

Mouth

Forelimb

Knee

Thigh

Claw

5 digits

3 digits

Hip

Hind limb

Lower leg

Claw

Foot

Animal tracks

ANIMAL TRACKS ARE TEMPORARY RECORDS of the passage of land animals across impressionable surfaces, such as damp sand, mud, or snow. By examining tracks noting the shape, size, and number of toes, claws, nails, hooves, or pads, it is often possible to identify the animal that made them. For example, the paw marks of mammals that walk on their toes, such as dogs and cats, can be differentiated by the shape and size of their pads. As well as identifying an animal, tracks can often reveal its way of life. For instance, the tracks made by web-footed ducks show that they are swimming birds, whereas the open-toed tracks of crows show that they are perching birds. In addition, the depth and pattern of tracks reveal whether the animal was walking, running, or hopping.

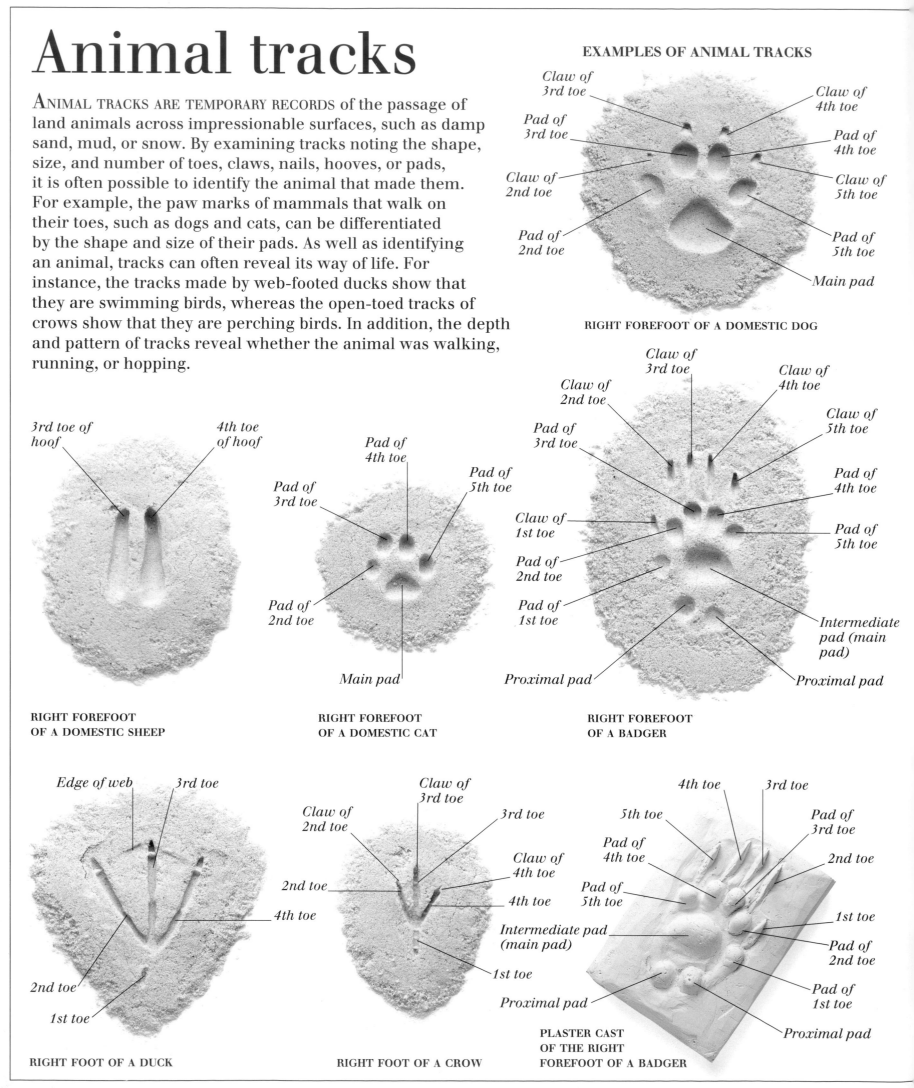

EXAMPLES OF ANIMAL TRACKS

Claw of 3rd toe
Pad of 3rd toe
Claw of 2nd toe
Pad of 2nd toe
Claw of 4th toe
Pad of 4th toe
Claw of 5th toe
Pad of 5th toe
Main pad

RIGHT FOREFOOT OF A DOMESTIC DOG

3rd toe of hoof
4th toe of hoof

RIGHT FOREFOOT OF A DOMESTIC SHEEP

Pad of 4th toe
Pad of 3rd toe
Pad of 5th toe
Pad of 2nd toe
Main pad

RIGHT FOREFOOT OF A DOMESTIC CAT

Claw of 3rd toe
Claw of 2nd toe
Pad of 3rd toe
Claw of 1st toe
Pad of 2nd toe
Pad of 1st toe
Proximal pad
Claw of 4th toe
Claw of 5th toe
Pad of 4th toe
Pad of 5th toe
Intermediate pad (main pad)
Proximal pad

RIGHT FOREFOOT OF A BADGER

Edge of web
3rd toe
2nd toe
4th toe
1st toe

RIGHT FOOT OF A DUCK

Claw of 3rd toe
Claw of 2nd toe
2nd toe
3rd toe
Claw of 4th toe
4th toe
1st toe

RIGHT FOOT OF A CROW

4th toe
5th toe
Pad of 4th toe
Pad of 5th toe
Intermediate pad (main pad)
Proximal pad
3rd toe
Pad of 3rd toe
2nd toe
1st toe
Pad of 2nd toe
Pad of 1st toe
Proximal pad

PLASTER CAST OF THE RIGHT FOREFOOT OF A BADGER

TRACKS AND MOVEMENT OF A HORSE

WALKING

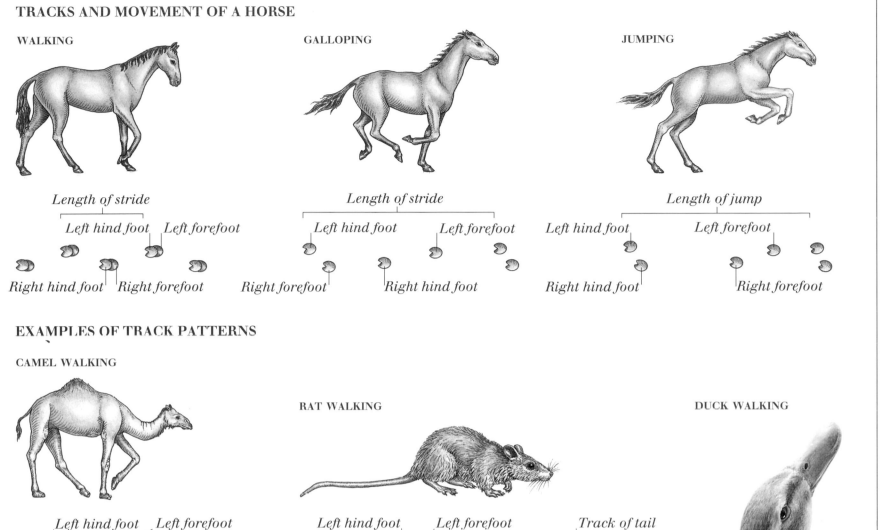

Length of stride

Left hind foot *Left forefoot*

Right hind foot *Right forefoot*

GALLOPING

Length of stride

Left hind foot *Left forefoot*

Right forefoot *Right hind foot*

JUMPING

Length of jump

Left hind foot *Left forefoot*

Right hind foot *Right forefoot*

EXAMPLES OF TRACK PATTERNS

CAMEL WALKING

Left hind foot *Left forefoot*

Right forefoot *Right hind foot*

RAT WALKING

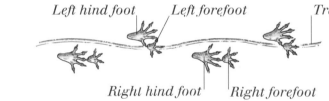

Left hind foot *Left forefoot* *Track of tail*

Right hind foot *Right forefoot*

DUCK WALKING

TOAD WALKING

Left hind foot *Left forefoot*

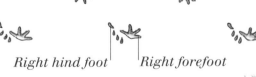

Right hind foot *Right forefoot*

Left foot

Right foot

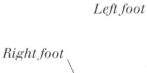

Animal classification

BIOLOGISTS USE A UNIVERSAL SYSTEM to classify animals and other organisms. All animals form one large grouping, the kingdom Animalia. The kingdom is subdivided into progressively smaller groups on the basis of similarities among animals within each group, and their differences from animals in other groups. The result of this repeated subdivision is a "family tree" of the animal world. First, the kingdom Animalia is divided into several phyla (singular: phylum)—for example, phylum Chordata, which includes all animals with backbones, such as birds, fish, and mammals. Each phylum is divided into classes, and each class into orders. Every order contains a number of families, each of which is split into genera (singular: genus). Finally, each genus is divided into species. In some cases, additional levels of classification may be used. These extra levels are indicated by prefixes, such as "super-" and "sub-". In addition to the formal biological classification, animals are often divided into two main groups: vertebrates and invertebrates. Vertebrates have a backbone (vertebral column), whereas invertebrates do not. The chart shows the main groups in the animal kingdom.

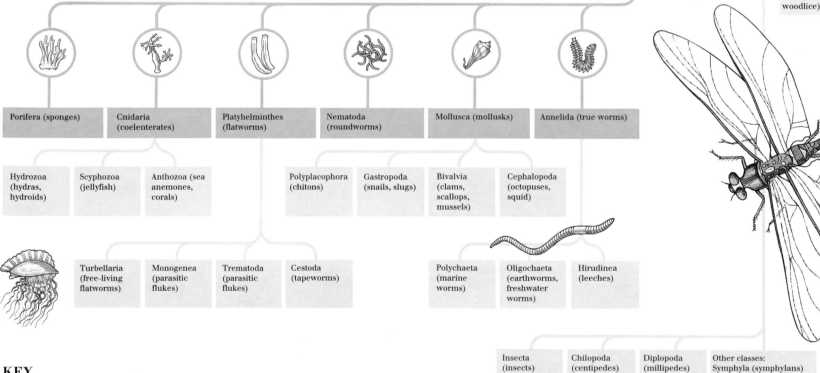

KINGDOM ANIMALIA

Uniramia (uniramians)

Malacostraca (lobsters, crabs, shrimps, woodlice)

Porifera (sponges)

Cnidaria (coelenterates)

Platyhelminthes (flatworms)

Nematoda (roundworms)

Mollusca (mollusks)

Annelida (true worms)

Hydrozoa (hydras, hydroids)

Scyphozoa (jellyfish)

Anthozoa (sea anemones, corals)

Polyplacophora (chitons)

Gastropoda (snails, slugs)

Bivalvia (clams, scallops, mussels)

Cephalopoda (octopuses, squid)

Turbellaria (free-living flatworms)

Monogenea (parasitic flukes)

Trematoda (parasitic flukes)

Cestoda (tapeworms)

Polychaeta (marine worms)

Oligochaeta (earthworms, freshwater worms)

Hirudinea (leeches)

Insecta (insects)

Chilopoda (centipedes)

Diplopoda (millipedes)

Other classes: Symphyla (symphylans) Pauropoda (pauropods)

KEY

These colors show the classification groupings used in the chart

PHYLUM

SUBPHYLUM

SUPERCLASS

CLASS

SUBCLASS

INFRACLASS

ORDER

Collembola (springtails)
Thysanura (silverfish, bristletails)
Ephemeroptera (mayflies)
Odonata (dragonflies, damselflies)
Isoptera (termites)
Orthoptera (locusts, crickets, grasshoppers, cockroaches, mantids)
Dermaptera (earwigs)
Phasmida (stick insects, leaf insects)
Psocoptera (book lice, bark lice)
Hemiptera (true bugs)

Anoplura (sucking lice)
Mallophaga (biting lice, bird lice)
Homoptera (white flies, aphids, scale insects, cicadas)
Coleoptera (beetles, weevils)
Neuroptera (alder flies, lacewings, ant lions, snake flies, dobsonflies)
Hymenoptera (ants, bees, wasps)
Siphonaptera (fleas)
Diptera (true flies, mosquitoes, gnats)
Lepidoptera (butterflies, moths)

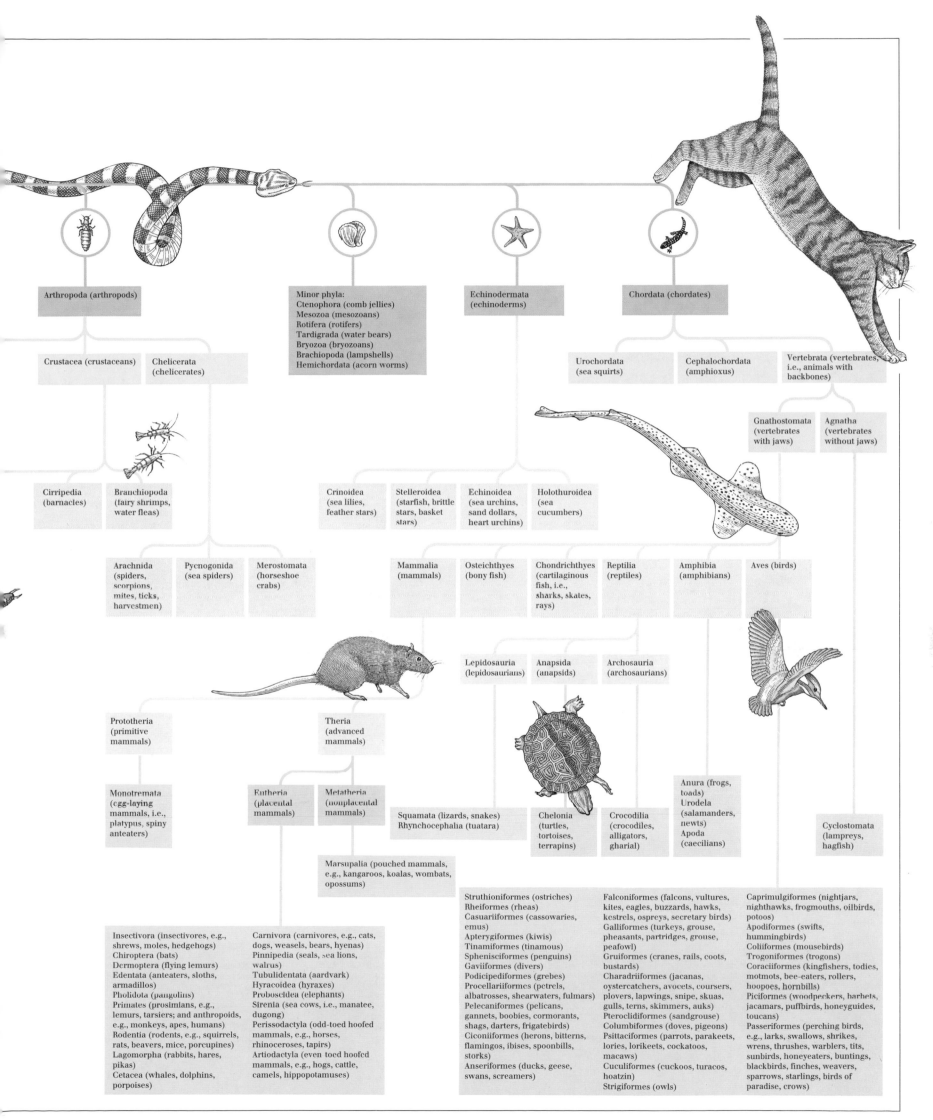

Arthropoda (arthropods)

Crustacea (crustaceans)

Chelicerata (chelicerates)

Cirripedia (barnacles)

Branchiopoda (fairy shrimps, water fleas)

Arachnida (spiders, scorpions, mites, ticks, harvestmen)

Pycnogonida (sea spiders)

Merostomata (horseshoe crabs)

Minor phyla:
Ctenophora (comb jellies)
Mesozoa (mesozoans)
Rotifera (rotifers)
Tardigrada (water bears)
Bryozoa (bryozoans)
Brachiopoda (lampshells)
Hemichordata (acorn worms)

Echinodermata (echinoderms)

Crinoidea (sea lilies, feather stars)

Stelleroidea (starfish, brittle stars, basket stars)

Echinoidea (sea urchins, sand dollars, heart urchins)

Holothuroidea (sea cucumbers)

Chordata (chordates)

Urochordata (sea squirts)

Cephalochordata (amphioxus)

Vertebrata (vertebrates, i.e., animals with backbones)

Gnathostomata (vertebrates with jaws)

Agnatha (vertebrates without jaws)

Mammalia (mammals)

Osteichthyes (bony fish)

Chondrichthyes (cartilaginous fish, i.e., sharks, skates, rays)

Reptilia (reptiles)

Amphibia (amphibians)

Aves (birds)

Lepidosauria (lepidosaurians)

Anapsida (anapsids)

Archosauria (archosaurians)

Prototheria (primitive mammals)

Theria (advanced mammals)

Monotremata (egg-laying mammals, i.e., platypus, spiny anteaters)

Eutheria (placental mammals)

Metatheria (nonplacental mammals)

Squamata (lizards, snakes)
Rhynchocephalia (tuatara)

Chelonia (turtles, tortoises, terrapins)

Crocodilia (crocodiles, alligators, gharial)

Anura (frogs, toads)
Urodela (salamanders, newts)
Apoda (caecilians)

Cyclostomata (lampreys, hagfish)

Marsupalia (pouched mammals, e.g., kangaroos, koalas, wombats, opossums)

Insectivora (insectivores, e.g., shrews, moles, hedgehogs)
Chiroptera (bats)
Dermoptera (flying lemurs)
Edentata (anteaters, sloths, armadillos)
Pholidota (pangolins)
Primates (prosimians, e.g., lemurs, tarsiers; and anthropoids, e.g., monkeys, apes, humans)
Rodentia (rodents, e.g., squirrels, rats, beavers, mice, porcupines)
Lagomorpha (rabbits, hares, pikas)
Cetacea (whales, dolphins, porpoises)

Carnivora (carnivores, e.g., cats, dogs, weasels, bears, hyenas)
Pinnipedia (seals, sea lions, walrus)
Tubulidentata (aardvark)
Hyracoidea (hyraxes)
Proboscidea (elephants)
Sirenia (sea cows, i.e., manatee, dugong)
Perissodactyla (odd-toed hoofed mammals, e.g., horses, rhinoceroses, tapirs)
Artiodactyla (even toed hoofed mammals, e.g., hogs, cattle, camels, hippopotamuses)

Struthioniformes (ostriches)
Rheiformes (rheas)
Casuariiformes (cassowaries, emus)
Apterygiformes (kiwis)
Tinamiformes (tinamous)
Sphenisciformes (penguins)
Gaviiformes (divers)
Podicipediformes (grebes)
Procellariiformes (petrels, albatrosses, shearwaters, fulmars)
Pelecaniformes (pelicans, gannets, boobies, cormorants, shags, darters, frigatebirds)
Ciconiiformes (herons, bitterns, flamingos, ibises, spoonbills, storks)
Anseriformes (ducks, geese, swans, screamers)

Falconiformes (falcons, vultures, kites, eagles, buzzards, hawks, kestrels, ospreys, secretary birds)
Galliformes (turkeys, grouse, pheasants, partridges, grouse, peafowl)
Gruiformes (cranes, rails, coots, bustards)
Charadriiformes (jacanas, oystercatchers, avocets, coursers, plovers, lapwings, snipe, skuas, gulls, terns, skimmers, auks)
Pteroclidiformes (sandgrouse)
Columbiformes (doves, pigeons)
Psittaciformes (parrots, parakeets, lories, lorikeets, cockatoos, macaws)
Cuculiformes (cuckoos, turacos, hoatzin)
Strigiformes (owls)

Caprimulgiformes (nightjars, nighthawks, frogmouths, oilbirds, potoos)
Apodiformes (swifts, hummingbirds)
Coliiformes (mousebirds)
Trogoniformes (trogons)
Coraciiformes (kingfishers, todies, motmots, bee-eaters, rollers, hoopoes, hornbills)
Piciformes (woodpeckers, barbets, jacamars, puffbirds, honeyguides, toucans)
Passeriformes (perching birds, e.g., larks, swallows, shrikes, wrens, thrushes, warblers, tits, sunbirds, honeyeaters, buntings, blackbirds, finches, weavers, sparrows, starlings, birds of paradise, crows)

59

Index

Acknowledgments

Dorling Kindersley would like to thank:
David Manning's Animal Ark; Intellectual Animals; Howletts Zoo, Canterbury; John Dunlop; Alexander O'Donnell; Sue Evans at the Royal Veterinary College, London; Dr Geoff Potts and Fred Frettsome at the Marine Biological Association of the United Kingdom, Plymouth; Jeremy Adams at the Booth Museum of Natural History, Brighton; Derek Telling at the Department of Anatomy, University of Bristol; the Natural History Museum, London; Andy Highfield at the Tortoise Trust; Brian Harris at the Aquarium, London Zoo; the Invertebrate Department, London Zoo; Dr Harold McClure at the Yerkes Regional Primate Research Center, Emory University, Atlanta, Georgia;

Nielson Lausen at the Harvard Medical School, New England Regional Primates Research Center, Southborough, Massachusetts; Dr Paul Hopwood at the Department of Veterinary Anatomy, University of Sydney; Dean Franklin; Roy Flooks

Additional photography:
Steve Gorton, Tim Ridley, Jane Burton, Matthew Ward, Jerry Young, Judith Harrington, Cyril Laubscher, Bob Langrish

Additional design assistance:
Simone End, Nicki Liddiard

Additional editorial assistance:
Christine Murdock, Louise Tucker

Illustrators:
John Woodcock, Simone End, David Hopkins, Sandra Pond, Nick Loates, Roy Flooks

Picture credits:
t=top b=bottom c=center l=left r=right
Oxford Scientific Films/Animals Animals/Breck P. Kent: 16cl; 25tl /London Scientific Films: 16tr; 17tc. Sinclair Stammers/Science Photo Library: 17cb

Index:
Irene Lyford

Picture research:
Clive Webster